From the
Housetops

From the Housetops

Preaching in the
Early Church and Today

Bruce E. Shields

Chalice Press®
St. Louis, Missouri

© Copyright 2000 by Bruce E. Shields

Bible quotations, unless otherwise noted, are from the *New Revised Standard Version Bible*, copyright 1989, Division of Christian Education of the National Council of the Churches of Christ in the United States of America. Used by permission. All rights reserved.

Cover: Dwane Carter
Interior design: Elizabeth Wright
Art direction: Michael Domínguez

This book is printed on acid-free, recycled paper.

Visit Chalice Press on the World Wide Web at
www.chalicepress.com

10 9 8 7 6 5 4 3 2 1   00 01 02 03

Library of Congress Cataloging–in–Publication Data

Shields, Bruce.
    From the housetops : preaching in the early church and today / Bruce
E. Shields.
         p.   cm.
    Includes bibliographical references.
    ISBN 0-8272-1031-0
1. Preaching—History I. Title.
BV4207 .S52   2000   00–010044
251—dc21

Printed in the United States of America

Contents

Preface

My purpose in writing this book is to make available to preachers and teachers of preaching the philosophy and tools of the study of oral communication. I contend that this approach can be helpful in understanding the New Testament and in preaching sermons in the twenty-first century that will approach the effectiveness of those preached in the first century. Therefore, I have resorted to summaries and simplifications of the work of scholars in orality studies, rhetoric, discourse analysis, philosophy of language, and even theology and biblical hermeneutics. While keeping the footnotes to a minimum, I include enough to help interested readers find more detailed and technical information on these subjects.

My interest in orality studies goes back two decades to a time when I discovered the writings of Walter Ong. The encouragement of his works, as well as an exchange of letters with him, have kept me on this track. I received a major boost along the way when I received a grant from the National Endowment for the Humanities in the summer of 1991 to participate in a seminar on the oral tradition in literature led by Dr. John Foley at the University of Missouri, Columbia.

Two sabbatical leaves from Emmanuel School of Religion have given me time for intense reading, reflection, and research. During the first of these, in 1989–90, I was able to study briefly in the Irish Folklore Library of the University of Dublin, Ireland. This experience put me in touch with the oral traditions and education processes of many of my own ancestors. During the second leave (1997), I was able to do research into the preaching styles of several non-Western cultures, including those of Romania, Malaysia, Korea, and Japan. All these experiences lie in the background of the book before you.

My doctoral dissertation in New Testament is a study of Paul's use of creation themes in Romans, an interest that grew out of my fascination with the preaching of Paul, especially his sermon on the Areopagus. My academic assignment at Emmanuel School of

Religion carries the title of Professor of Preaching and Biblical Hermeneutics. I also teach courses in worship. Thus, I see myself as a Jack-of-many-trades and a master of none. Yet I would have it no other way. The preacher, especially in our postmodern era, must be a generalist, and I am committed to preparing women and men to be the best preachers they can be.

Therefore, I offer this work to help people become effective communicators of the gospel that Jesus whispered in the ears of his disciples and which they subsequently shouted from the housetops.

My thanks go to Emmanuel School of Religion, the National Endowment for the Humanities, and my students, especially Valmir Delgado and Michael Tanner, who helped me to organize and proofread the book.

Most of all, to my patient-enough and loving wife, Rosemarie; to our offspring, Karen, James, and Robert, who have survived my preaching and lecturing and who continue to encourage me anyway; and to our granddaughters, Elizabeth Grace and Alexandra Jeanette, who help me to stay human—thank you.

Introduction

The Concept of This Book

This book is an attempt to analyze representative texts of the New Testament to discern the oral communication that lies behind them and to find a way to relate those methods and forms of communication to the ministry of preaching to today's hearers.

Its central thesis is that from a study of the communication of the earliest Christians we can learn to proclaim the gospel effectively in our present situations. This does not mean that we should borrow first-century forms of speech and transplant them into our pulpits. It means, rather, that as the early church used forms familiar to its hearers with which to communicate its message, so we preachers should study how effective communication occurs in our cultural settings and use those forms in appropriate ways in our preaching.

The book is designed to investigate selected works from the New Testament to discern signs of oral communication in them, to distill from that study an understanding of the nature and central focus of early Christian communication, and to apply these findings wherever possible to the task of Christian communication today. The following survey of the history of human communication should serve as background material for the study that comprises the twelve chapters of the book.

A Little History

The first four hundred years in the life of the church were characterized by what Walter Ong calls "primary orality."[1] By this term he describes cultures that, even in the presence of writing, remain dependent on the spoken and heard word for the most important kinds of communication. The development of means of communication progressed very slowly for the first four million years or so of human history. By whatever process human speech

---

[1]This terminology can be found in several of Ong's works, but it is most helpfully described and illustrated in the chapter "Some Psychodynamics of Orality," in his *Orality and Literacy* (New York: Methuen, 1982), 31–77.

developed, for several millennia communication was confined to direct speech, supplemented by gestures, fires, drums, and horns. Early forms of pictorial representation of things and events appear to have been developed in all ancient cultures. Writing as we know it seems to have been introduced first in Sumer around 3500 B.C.E., with the phonetic alphabet being developed in Phoenicia around 800 B.C.E. This development gave people a way to represent sounds instead of just objects and events. Obviously, hand copying made any mass communication very slow and labor-intensive. The first practical mass production of literature became possible with the invention of block printing, which appeared in Rome around 131 C.E. and in Asia about three centuries later.[2] Ong convincingly argues that Gutenberg's development of moveable-type printing in mid-fifteenth-century Germany made the written word considerably more common, with the result that a large enough percentage of the population learned to read and write to allow us to characterize the culture as primarily literate.[3] It is understandable, then, that Martin Luther appears, with all his learning, to have remained basically an oral person, while one generation later John Calvin would view the written word as the primary guarantee of orthodoxy. In many ways Luther can be considered a modern thinker, and he used the printing press to great advantage; but he appears to have retained the criterion of the oral *regula fidei*, which he inherited from the medieval church, while Calvin was guided more by the Renaissance concern for ancient texts.[4]

The European Enlightenment of the seventeenth and eighteenth centuries was the source of the next impetus toward dependence on the written word in Western civilization. Our worldview and thought patterns are so determined by this culture of literacy that it is difficult for us even to recognize it, much less to analyze it. Like the air we breathe, we take it for granted until somebody calls our attention to it. However, the rapid changes in communication at the end of the twentieth century are getting our attention. Terms like *modem, baud*, and *e-mail* have become commonplace. (Oddly enough, the word "commonplace" is a term

---

[2]See the summary of this history in William F. Fore, *Mythmakers: Gospel, Culture, and the Media* (New York: Friendship Press, 1990), 34–35.

[3]Ong, *The Presence of the Word: Some Prolegomena for Cultural and Religious History* (New Haven, Conn.: Yale University Press, 1967; Minneapolis: University of Minnesota Press, 1981), 47ff.

[4]For a good discussion of Luther in this regard, see William A. Graham, *Beyond the Written Word: Oral Aspects of Scripture in the History of Religion* (Cambridge: Cambridge University Press, 1987), 141–54. I will quote Calvin on the written word below, page 38.

from oral education.) Those of us who did not grow up getting most of our information about the world from television and computers, but rather from books and newspapers, often find ourselves a bit dizzy in today's world. Being involved in such a shift should make it somewhat easier for us to understand that a similar shift happened, although much more slowly, in the change from primary orality to primary literacy.

That change was not just a development of new technology; it eventually changed the way people thought. The shift from the use of narrative to define the individual, the tribe, and, more recently, the nation to more linear, "logical" definitions indicates a profound change in self-awareness. The more oral and narrative-dependent a culture is, the more community orientation one discovers there; whereas the more literary and linear a culture is, the more individualistic is its thinking. I am aware that such a generalization is open to question from many sides, but it seems defensible as a general rule, and I mention it to indicate that the shift we are now undergoing will likely mean an equally profound change in the way our descendants think about themselves and the world.

Since one purpose of preaching is to offer people a vocabulary by which they can better express and therefore understand reality as including dimensions of divinity and eternity and to identify themselves as persons under the reign of God, such a developing change in the patterns of thinking is of vital importance to us as preachers. We who are dedicated to the ministry of reconciliation, a primary aspect of which is helping people to develop new ways of recognizing and dealing with reality, must be alert to the patterns of thought that our prevailing culture teaches us to use. Regardless of the age to which people tend to conform (see Rom. 12:1–2), the characteristics of that age must be recognized if transformation by the renewing of the mind (repentance) is to take place. For the preacher, such awareness is doubly important: By it we can learn what we are up against, and from it we can learn the most effective means of communication.

As recipients of the culture of the Enlightenment and therefore as primarily literate thinkers, we preachers and teachers of preaching at the end of the twentieth century find ourselves in many cases conceiving of the sermon as a document, that is, as a set of written symbols on a page, which will then be read, with more or less directness, either off the page or from memory, to a silent audience. Thus, we "finish" a sermon one day in a given week and "deliver" it to a congregation on Sunday. "Preparation and delivery" seems to be a commodity-oriented way of thinking about preaching, and it is hard to imagine a first-century Christian thinking in those terms. This pattern of thought is, in fact, typical of a literate culture, a culture like the one often referred to as eighteenth- and nineteenth-century civilization. In that culture the printed word was the primary medium of mass communication. Scientific discoveries were heralded, revolutions fomented, and governments directed by means of the printed page. The familiar dictum of the nineteenth century that the pen is mightier than the sword[5] made sense only when the written word could be broadly disseminated by printing and mailing. This statement, which is often connected to Thomas Jefferson, is certainly underscored by his letter to Colonel Edward Carrington in January of 1787:

> The basis of our government being the opinion of the people, the very first object should be to keep that right; and were it left to me to decide whether we should have a government without newspapers, or newspapers without a government, I should not hesitate a moment to choose the latter.[6]

Newspaper and journal editors of the eighteenth and nineteenth centuries wielded great power. The sermons of preachers like Charles Haddon Spurgeon were printed and shipped all over the world almost as soon as they were preached. Many of the best-known leaders in both politics and religion during that time published their own pamphlets or journals, as is seen in the work of Thomas Paine and others. Alexander Campbell, who commanded large audiences all over the United States between 1836 and 1856, built that following by his judicious use of the printing press.

To this author, it seems important to learn all we can about the communication process of the apostolic church in order to check our own strategies of communication. Let us seek to learn from those early believers how we can make an impact on our world.

---

[5]Edward B. Lytton, in *Richelieu*, Act II, Scene 2. Cited in John Bartlett, *Familiar Quotations,* 13th ed. (Boston: Little, Brown, 1955), 510.

[6]Cited in John Bartlett, *Familiar Quotations,* 13th ed. (Boston: Little, Brown, 1955), 373.

1

Language and the Word of God

How often we hear it said that Christianity is a "religion of the book"! Is this really an accurate portrayal of early Christianity? There is little argument against such a characterization of many forms of Christianity during the past century and a half. But is Christianity in its essence dependent on a book? My thesis in this work is that as important as the Christian scriptures are for the evangelization of the world and the edification of believers, the formation and essence of Christianity are more closely linked to the spoken word than to the written word.

The simple facts of Christian history testify to this. The church was established and flourished throughout the Roman Empire of the first century before the New Testament documents were written in their entirety and certainly before they were gathered into one book. Thus, it is clear that Christianity predates its special book and, therefore, is not dependent on it.

On the other hand, it is my contention that H. H. Farmer was correct when he wrote:

From the beginning, then, Christianity, being concerned with The Event which by definition has no parallel, God being agent in it as He is not in other happenings, was committed to preaching, to proclamation. Whoso said Christianity, said preaching. There was no choice between

5

that and absolutely ceasing to be, without the least chance of ever occurring again.[1]

The primary means of communication in the early church was speech. Those earliest Christians revered and used the Hebrew Scriptures, especially in their Greek translation (the Septuagint, abbreviated LXX). But for several centuries even the writings of the early church indicate that written documents are seen as helpful, but not as primary in the work of the church. In the late fourth century, Ambrose, bishop of Milan, wrote in his *Commentary on St. Luke* (4:5), "Everything we believe, we believe either through sight or through hearing." And from his standpoint in a primarily oral culture, he continues, "Sight is often deceived, hearing serves as guarantee."[2]

During the first three hundred years or more of its existence, Christianity was understood as a faith born of and nourished by the spoken word. In fact, many important thinkers and leaders throughout the history of the church have recognized the primacy and the power of speech. From fourth-century Egypt "there is evidence that many of the desert fathers believed that too much reliance on books, even the most sacred, could lead to trouble."[3] Both Martin Luther and John Wesley could be quoted in this regard. It was only with the development of moveable-type printing and the concurrent expansion of literacy in the nations of the Western hemisphere that the written word became primary, and people began to think of language in terms of symbols occupying space on a line of writing instead of sounds uttered and lost in time. We who live in an age of quickly changing means of communication should be eager to consider the orality of early Christianity and even of the Bible itself. This consideration is a primary focus of this book.

A second and not less important aim is to relate the spoken word of faith to God, the object of that faith. It is not my purpose here to develop a complete theology of the word. However, it seems important at the outset of this work to discuss some of the

---

[1]H. H. Farmer, *The Servant of the Word* (Digswell Place, England: James Nisbet & Co. 1941), 18–19.

[2]Cited in Ong, *The Presence of the Word*, 52–53.

[3]Douglas Burton-Christie, *The Word in the Desert: Scripture and the Quest for Holiness in Early Christian Monasticism* (New York: Oxford University Press, 1992), 115.

primary points at which theology of the word and preaching the word intersect. In these paragraphs, then, I propose to summarize some important thinking on the subject in the latter half of the twentieth century and to put these thoughts together in a way that will stimulate our thinking in new directions and thus encourage us in the task of preaching.

What Is the Word?

The question at the outset is, What do we mean when we use the expression the "word of God?" How can human language be the word of God?

Frederick Buechner has described beautifully how the gospel functions as tragedy, as comedy, and finally as fairy tale.[4] Fairy tales invariably include magic: the kiss of the prince, the name of Rumpelstiltskin, the wand of the godmother, the shoes of the witch, the incantation of the sorcerer. There is very limited value in comparing either the Bible or Christian preaching to fairy tales, but coming as they do from oral cultures, fairy tales illustrate an understanding of language that our literacy has caused us to lose sight of. We relegate enchanted (note *chant* in the term) acts and words to the realm of superstition, and superstition is a way of thinking that is beneath the dignity of our enlightened minds.

However, the Bible deals with word, that is, language, as more than symbol, sign, or code, as most modern analyses of communication explain it. Are we forced to choose between contemporary communication theory and the primitive or naive magical treatment of language in the Bible? Must we discard the living word of Hebrews 4:12 along with the three-story universe cosmology of the biblical world? Perhaps not.

There are voices today calling our attention to a much deeper element in language than its function as a symbol or a code system. They do not deny that words function as symbols, but they urge us to consider also the necessity, the power, and the "magic" of language.[5]

---

[4]Frederick Buechner, *Telling The Truth* (New York: Harper & Row, 1977).

[5]See the book by the Jesuit Thomas M. King, *Enchantments: Religion and the Power of the Word* (Kansas City, Mo.: Sheed & Ward, 1989); one by a Nobel chemist, Ilya Prigogine and Isabelle Stenger, *Order Out of Chaos* (New York: Bantam, 1984); and one by a historian of science, Morris Berman, *The Reenchantment of the World* (New York: Bantam, 1985).

Hans-Georg Gadamer, in his seminal work *Wahrheit und Methode (Truth and Method)*[6] shows the limited nature of the sign theory of language. He argues that this understanding arises when we begin and end our analysis of language "with the medium—the words,"[7] thus observing its function only between the minds of sender and receiver. He maintains that there is no break in the continuum of experience, thinking, understanding, and communication; they are all linguistic acts.[8] He proceeds to argue that we do not communicate mere individual thoughts or events with words but also the world in which event and thought are at home. Furthermore, "in and through [language] comes the possibility of having world at all."[9] How else could we be taken seriously when we talk about expressing ourselves? Paul Ricoeur[10] explores some of these same paths when in his interpretive scheme he insists that the text be permitted to interpret the interpreter. Such an expectation presupposes a life inherent in the word itself.

No matter how far we are willing to pursue the "magic" inherent in language, we must recognize a real power there. Words evoke not just objective images or concepts, but also deep emotions. John Wesley was one of many preachers who have marveled at the impact of words that came from their mouths. He describes what happened to a hostile mob when he began to preach: "They were amazed, they were ashamed; they were melted down; they devoured every word. What a turn was this!"[11] And we are not hard-pressed to identify those who have used language for negative ends. An Adolf Hitler could stir sinful passions and mislead hosts of otherwise decent people. Jim Jones and his ilk continually remind us of this danger. Modern political and advertising establishments are only too aware of the power of the word.

Furthermore, it appears that language is necessary for human survival. The word is the means by which we transcend our individual beings and construct cultures and civilizations—the

---

[6]Hans-Georg Gadamer, *Wahrheit und Methode* (Tübingen: J. C. B. Mohr, 1975); English translation, *Truth and Method*, trans. G. Borden and J. Cumming (New York: Seabury Press, 1975).

[7]Ibid., 390.

[8]Richard E. Palmer, *Hermeneutics* (Evanston, Ill.: Northwestern University Press, 1969), 203.

[9]Gadamer, *Truth*, 419.

[10]For a good introduction see Paul Ricoeur, *Essays on Biblical Interpretation* (Philadelphia: Fortress Press, 1980).

[11]John Wesley, *Journal* (Chicago: Moody Press, 1951), 169. Cited in John R. W. Stott, *Between Two Worlds* (Grand Rapids, Mich.: Eerdmans, 1982), 106.

medium by which we reach out to the other and are reached by that other. The alternative is mere physical existence in the loneliness of silence. But language permits us to assign significance to life. The word is necessary to the life we label human.

Thus, we see that word is more than mere sign or symbol used to encode thought. Word is necessary. Word has a peculiar power over persons. And word participates somehow in the magic of experience, thought, and understanding.

We are discussing not just a philosophy of the word, but more—we need a theology of the word. Thus, we must address the question, What sort of *theos* (God) is found in a *logos* (word)?

Who Is the God of the Word?

Our God is the creator of communication. We err when we think or act as though the human race has done God a favor by getting in touch with him. The voice of Karl Barth should continually remind us of the direction of revelation—it is not discovered, but heard or received. This communication comes to us from God. Along with other wonders in earthly existence, "Scripture, too, stands in that indirect identity of human existence with God himself, which is conditioned neither by the nature of God nor that of man [*sic*], but brought about by the decision and act of God."[12] For this reason Barth could write in his preface to his *The Epistle to the Romans*, "Were I driven to choose between [the historical-critical method] and the venerable doctrine of Inspiration, I should without hesitation adopt the latter, which has a broader, deeper, more important justification."[13] We should, of course, employ every possible means to enhance our human understanding of the word, but we should never forget that it comes from the God who created even our ability to understand and communicate.

Our God is also the healer of broken communication. Standing with Barth as one of our century's major word of God theologians, Anders Nygren emphasized *agape* (love) as the dominating motif of Christianity.[14] Nygren's theology is problematic in many ways,[15]

---

[12]Karl Barth, *Church Dogmatics* I, 2, *The Doctrine of the Word of God*, trans. G. T. Thomson and Harold Knight, (Edinburgh: T. & T. Clark, 1963).

[13]Karl Barth, *The Epistle to the Romans*, trans. E. C. Hoskyns (Oxford: Oxford University Press, 1975), 1.

[14]Anders Nygren, *Agape and Eros*, trans. P. S. Watson (Philadelphia: Westminster Press, 1953).

[15]See Gustav Wingren, *Theology in Conflict*, trans., E. H. Wahlstrom (Philadelphia: Muhlenberg Press, 1958), 85–107.

but it does draw our attention to the deep desire of our God of the word to restore the communication broken by sin. More recently, motif research has examined the theme of reconciliation, which is even more directly relevant to the characteristics of God as healer.[16] Thus, we are reminded that God is not just the One who created communication but also the One who continually enables us to hear and to speak. God does this as the healer of broken relationships, both vertical and horizontal.

We rarely think of the Omnipotent as having to run any risks. But in our own experience, we discover that nobody acts as a peacemaker—a communication restorer—without risking his or her own reputation and relationships. This is doubly true when, in order to heal, we must reveal ourselves, especially to persons who are clearly unstable. The scriptures give us, however, a rather clear picture of God running the risk of revealing Godself to people who have shown themselves as unfaithful. The cross is, of course, the symbol of the ultimate risk, and the Gethsemane scene shows the reality of the risk. There are no halfway measures here—no "cheap grace," as Dietrich Bonhoeffer pointed out. Here is also where one of Bonhoeffer's most important emphases comes in, that our God is the God of the center—not of the gaps.[17]

The Christian message is that the God of the word is a God who was not above getting those divine hands dirty—a God who created beings with whom God could communicate, a God who in love acted to reconcile those beings who had broken the communication, a God who shed sweat and blood to heal us. In the words of Colossians 1:22, "[you] he has now reconciled in his fleshly body through death, so as to present you holy and blameless and irreproachable before him."

What Is the Word of God?

Only as we awaken to the possibilities of the word as such and become aware of the God of the word can we begin either to understand or to appreciate what it means to talk about the word of God. The claim that this God has spoken makes all the difference in the world. Barth writes:

---

[16]Cf. Ralph Martin, *Reconciliation: A Study of Paul's Theology* (Atlanta: John Knox Press, 1981); and Peter Stuhlmacher, *Das Evangelium von der Versöhnung in Christus* (Stuttgart: Calwer Verlag, 1979).

[17]Dietrich Bonhoeffer, *Ethics*, trans. N. H. Smith (New York: Macmillan, 1962), 83f.; and *The Cost of Discipleship*, trans. R. H. Fuller (New York: Macmillan, 1961), 35ff.

The subject of theology is the history of the communion of God with man [*sic*] and of man with God. This history is proclaimed, in ancient times and today, in the Old and New Testaments. The message of the Christian Church has its origin and its contents in this history. The subject of theology is, in this sense, the "Word of God."[18]

The breathtaking scope of the word of God is vividly portrayed in hundreds of pages of Barth's writings. But only in his preaching by means of his dialectic does he escape an inherent tendency to otherworldliness. At this point he runs counter to the consistent witness of the Bible—a witness with which Emil Brunner is more compatible. Brunner describes truth as a divine-human encounter.[19] Just as our speaking is not only an encoding of thought but also an expression of ourselves, so God encounters us in word. When we consider carefully the nature of God, we realize that a direct and full encounter with the Divine would be more than the human individual could survive. Therefore, the word of God implies that God has decided, for our benefit, to reveal Godself indirectly and in a limited way. Human language might seem to be a poor vehicle for divine expression, since it is culturally determined and as fallible as the human mind. Yet God has chosen to use this vehicle to encounter us fallible creatures in our cultural environment.

Thus, in a way God has chosen to put the divine self-expression at the mercy of human reason and inquiry.[20] Most of us feel (correctly, I think!) responsible to use the same canons and methods of understanding on the Bible that we use on other historical texts. Literary and historical criticism should not be the totality of our hermeneutic, but they certainly form an important part. As incongruous as it may seem, God's revelation has been given to us in a form that invites (one could say, demands) our critique—our tools and power of analysis.

Furthermore, this word of God is a divine revelation, which we human beings can speak. Indeed, we who have experienced the encounter—we who have really heard—may or rather *must* speak it. In a letter to his professor, Adolf von Harnack, Barth

---

[18]Karl Barth, *Dogmatics in Outline*, trans. G. T. Thomson (New York: Harper, 1959), 5.

[19]Emil Brunner, *Truth as Encounter*, trans. A. M. Loos and D. Cairns (Philadelphia: Westminster Press, 1964), 21ff.

[20]See the critique of Barth, Brunner, and Bultmann on this point in John Macquarrie, *Twentieth-Century Religious Thought* (New York: Charles Scribner's Sons, 1981), 333f.

wrote that the task of theology "is one with the task of preaching; it consists in taking up and passing on the word of Christ."[21] Thus, the theology of the word is the basis of Christian preaching. The transcendent becomes immanent by entrusting divinity to our words, which when we hear correctly we hear as the very word of Christ, and thus the hearing of the word awakens faith in the hearer.[22]

Seeing, then, the importance of our developing a theological conception of language and seeing also the potential of such thinking to improve our preaching of God's word, we need to give some consideration to the process of thinking about a theology of the word of God. Where do we begin?

Toward a Theology of the Word

If the Creator of the universe has revealed or is revealing Godself, it would seem quite illogical to begin any thinking process without taking that into account. Thus, if revelation has happened or is happening, it seems a waste of time to try to build an understanding of *any* word—and especially of God's word—by beginning from the human side and working toward God. I recognize this assertion is debatable, but it seems to me that beginning from the human side would be a work of philosophical creativity; it would depend on our logic and experience. But if God has revealed Godself, then the task before us is not philosophical creativity, but investigation, description, interpretation, and proclamation (not to mention obedience). In such an investigation, our philosophical or theological questioning should focus on the process of revelation: its means, its reception, and its effects.

We might ask what language God speaks. This question should not be lightly dismissed as facetious. For if, as we are told, language is culturally determined, then anything God would say could be understood by human hearers only on the basis of our limited universe of meaning. Thus, God is faced not only with the challenge of communicating infinitude to finite human minds, but God is also faced with the staggering problem of communicating in many different language systems. For the theist there is no insurmountable difficulty in conceiving of God's

---

[21]Karl Barth, *Theologische Fragen und Antworten*, 10ff., trans. and cited by Macquarrie, *Twentieth-Century Religious Thought*, 321.

[22]Romans 10:17, with which we shall deal more fully below.

revelation, but for the cross-cultural communicator of God's word it becomes a daily challenge.

However, for our purpose it is more important to wonder about the nature of God's self-revelation by word. Anybody involved in communication knows the frustration of discovering that hearers have not understood or have misunderstood. This experience in part prompted a movement among biblical theologians some time ago to put the main emphasis on God's acts, rather than on God's words. The difficulty of this movement proved to be that events are even more ambiguous as bearers of revelation than are words. Therefore, some astute students of scripture had to point out to the theological world that the scriptures claim to transmit revelation in word, not only as interpretation of events but also as direct address from God to human beings.[23]

Helmut Thielicke insists that word is the only medium available for direct divine revelation. After discussing the ambiguities of events, he observes:

> All this points to the fact that we can speak of revelation in the strict sense only when the author of revelation manifests himself in, if we will, "absolute directness," i.e., only when he is identical with the mode of his manifestation. This holds true, however, only of his Word. God is his Word, or, better, he makes himself identical with it (John 1:1). In the word of his self-presentation ("I am who I will be," Exodus 3:14), in the word of the covenant ("I am the Lord your God," Exodus 20:2; Deuteronomy 6:4; cf. Exodus 3:15; 6:2), and in the word of salvation and judgment as it is laid upon the prophets, he makes himself directly present. He is wholly in his word. Even when the reference is to his glory (*kavod*), name (*shem*), or countenance (*panim*), he is attested as the one who presents himself in his Word.[24]

If we are to turn from abstract thought about divine revelation to a consideration of both the Bible and Christian preaching, we

---

[23]See James Barr, "Revelation through History in the Old Testament and in Modern Theology," *Princeton Seminary Bulletin* 56 (1963): 4–14; and compare his "Story and History in Biblical Theology," in *The Scope and Authority of the Bible* (Philadelphia: Westminster Press, 1980).

[24]Helmut Thielicke, *The Evangelical Faith,* vol. 2 (Grand Rapids, Mich.: Eerdmans, 1977), 12.

must ask at this point, What happens when the human memory of divine oral communication is changed from oral to written form? The form critics have been dealing with this question on one level for some time, but only recently have anthropologists, communication experts, and scholars of literature begun to examine one another's disciplines closely enough to approach this issue at a deeper level than that of mere forms.[25] Since preaching completes this circle, it is important for preachers to consider the whole process. The preacher is to take a written text that was once an oral communication and communicate it orally.[26]

Several strictly hermeneutical questions arise here. Is it possible to investigate such a word objectively? How does our human interpretation affect this word? We cannot here develop a whole hermeneutic, but we should recognize a central issue of theology: God's identifying Godself with the word is part of the risk that God took in the process of self-revelation. God placed Godself at the disposal of human beings. We can (and for those of us who recognize God in the word, we *must*) investigate it, in spite of all the risks such an undertaking implies, since the investigation of God's word is the means to contemplation of God. God can be misunderstood and God's word can be misapplied, but apparently that is better than being ignored.

One final question in regard to the word of God is directly homiletical: Is proclamation about that word or is it part of it? Is the preacher to speak about God's word—explain it, apply it? Or is our commission to "preach the word" in the sense that our preaching somehow becomes the word of God? This question will remain before us as we continue.

It is clear that words do not so much implant meaning in the mind of the receiver as they elicit meaning from the fund of understanding already present. Thus, any discussion of communication must consider the hearer. To a great extent we hear what we are willing to hear, and we sometimes arrange not to hear things that we prefer to ignore. Thielicke writes:

---

[25]Note the work of Walter Ong, *The Presence of the Word; Rhetoric, Romance, and Technology* (Ithaca, N.Y.: Cornell University Press, 1971); *Interfaces of the Word: Studies in the Evolution of Consciousness and Culture* (Ithaca, N.Y.: Cornell University Press, 1977); and his more summarizing work, *Orality and Literacy*. In the next chapter I introduce more fully this interdisciplinary work.

[26]See Rudolf Bohren, *Predigtlehre* (Munich: Christian Kaiser Verlag, 1980), 148: "Communication research reminds exegesis of its immediate goal: the texts should become again what they were, spoken word, preached sermon" (au. trans.).

> Failure to accept the revelation of God has its basis...in that man [*sic*] has surrendered himself to untruth, that he no longer praised God, that he is not grateful to him (Rom. 1:21), that he no longer understands himself in his creatureliness (Rom. 3:4; Eph. 4:25), and that he loves darkness more than light (Jn. 3:19).[27]

He goes on to point out that this refusal to hear actually turns revelation on its head. "God is made in the image of man (Rom. 1:23)."[28]

On the positive side, the Bible describes some persons as conditioned or disposed to receiving revelation. Schools of prophets and disciples of Jesus as well as many individuals desired and expected a word from God. Yet none of this indicates that revelation is contingent on any person's status. Both Moses and Saul of Tarsus are examples of persons who were exceptionally well prepared to do what God wanted them to do and at the same time were diametrically opposed to the sort of word spoken to them. The revelation got through in spite of the hearers.

The biblical understanding is not that faith is the prerequisite to reception of God's word but rather is the result of hearing. Romans 4:18–21 shows Abraham hearing a word both unexpected and unbelievable, humanly speaking. But recognizing God as its source he believed, "being fully convinced that God was able to do what he had promised" (v. 21). So faith is taking God at God's word.

This means that hearing the gospel is the means to faith. Romans 10:17 says precisely that. Of course, hearing in this sense (*akoe* = *shema*) is more than an act of perception; it includes also the readiness to obey what is heard.

The starting point, then, for our theology of the word is the recognition that, as in any other language event, both the sender (in this case, God) and the receiver are fully involved in the process. How do we proceed?

Toward a Dynamic Word

Any intelligent communication is a process with inherent power; but the word of God is a peculiarly dynamic word. As students of history, we should recognize the dangers of holding a

---

[27]Thielicke, *Evangelical Faith*, 6.
[28]Ibid., 16.

static concept of God's word. The absurdities of allegorism as well as the rigidities of scholasticism were founded on the assumption that the Bible, the Bible alone, and the Bible in every minute detail was *the* word of God. The search that continues in some quarters for theological significance in every single word or letter of the biblical documents is symptomatic of a peculiar failure among sincere believers to grasp the real power of the word of God.

The scriptures view God's word dynamically. It is the word that brings the creation into being. "And God said..." (Gen. 1). "The God who...calls into existence the things that do not exist" (Rom. 4:17b). God's name is revealed to Moses to begin the process of freeing the Hebrews from Egypt, and that exodus was understood as a response to the word of God. "Out of Egypt I called my son" (Hos. 11:1b). The prophets consistently and insistently claimed that God had spoken a word to them and that the word should change the course of history. And of course the identification of Jesus as the *logos* of God incarnate is the climax of this dynamic view of God's word. We have been instructed often enough that *dabar* (Hebrew for *word*) in the Old Testament is used to include both symbol and act, both utterance and event. Thus, "word" in the Old Testament is more than code—it has content. The New Testament use of *logos*, especially in John 1, and even of *rhema* in Romans 10:17 appears to carry over this concept of language.[29]

In the light of this usage (and especially the Rom. 10:17 passage), we should not hesitate to connect the word of God directly with preaching. Gerhard Ebeling defined the word of God as "the movement which leads from the text of holy scripture to the sermon."[30] Bonhoeffer wrote, "The proclaimed word is the incarnate Christ himself,... not a medium of expression for something else, something which lies behind it, but rather it is the Christ himself, walking through his congregation as the Word."[31] Thus, we see that preaching can be viewed as more than talk about God's word; it is also the word of God.

Since the hearer is so much a part of the process of communication, the theologian of the word must concern himself or

---

[29]See Hans van der Geest, *Presence in the Pulpit* (Atlanta: John Knox Press, 1982), 83, and Gerhard von Rad, *Old Testament Theology* (New York: Harper & Row, 1962), 80ff.

[30]Gerhard Ebeling, *Word and Faith*, trans. James W. Leitch (Philadelphia: Fortress Press, 1963), 311.

[31]Dietrich Bonhoeffer, *Gesamelte Schriften IV*, 240; cited by Clyde Fant, *Worldly Preaching* (Nashville: Thomas Nelson, 1975), 107f.

herself with human understanding—with hermeneutics. In fact, the sort of process theology of the word that we have been considering points to vital links between hermeneutics and homiletics. If taking the Bible seriously means, as we have suggested, preaching the word, then hermeneutics and homiletics are interdependent. Hermeneutics without homiletics in view (and ultimately in practice) cannot claim to be the interpretation of the word of God—it is merely an analysis of a static word resulting in a static report. On the other hand, homiletics without careful hermeneutics is always in danger of merely producing neat reports of a preacher's views on a subject, and thus it has no hope of sharing the dynamic of the Divine.

On the positive side, this approach makes both hermeneutics and homiletics valid and vital theological disciplines. Theology itself—whether biblical, historical, or systematic—remains a static discipline without the work of both interpretation and preaching. It is, therefore, important for the future of the whole theological enterprise that we develop an understanding of language and preaching that is both biblical and contemporary.

A dynamic understanding of hermeneutics and homiletics together appears to our view in Romans 10:17. The exegetical key to the verse seems to be the meaning of *rhematos* (word). Although I hesitate to limit my understanding of *word* (language) to a code or symbol system, it must be recognized that words are functional. They are more than objects to be understood. Rather, they function to make something else (an event, thought, concept, person) understood. To put it differently, words function hermeneutically; they are agents or means of understanding. In Romans 10:17 *rhema* appears with *dia* (the preposition "through" or "by means of"), as the agent of *akoe* (hearing/understanding)! *Christou* (of Christ) is (not atypically) ambiguous. It could indicate either a word about Christ or Christ's word—or, as I tend increasingly to think, both. In the statement from Isaiah 53:1 that Paul quotes in verse 16, "Lord, who has believed our message?" the word translated as *message* is a form of the Hebrew word *shema* and so could be translated, "what we have heard." The LXX translates it with the Greek word *rhema*, which Paul then picks up in his summary statement in verse 17, where he uses both *akoe* and *rhema*, which emphasizes the hearing of both the communicator and the audience.

Paul's claim here is that the faith on which our reception of God's justification is based arises from the hearing (attention to, understanding of, and submission to) made possible by means of Christ's word. This word is interpretive of the reality that is Christ, that is, it is revelatory. And the context makes it clear that Paul is thinking about Christian preaching. We shall return to this text in chapter 10.

We could call many other biblical texts to the fore to guide the process of our development of a theology of the dynamic word. A close look at 2 Corinthians 4 and 5 should be rewarding. I suspect, however, that virtually every investigation of this kind would discover a strong emphasis on the dynamic nature of God's word and the vital role of interpretation and preaching in the whole process of revelation.

Where Does That Leave Us?

In the final analysis we are dealing with *our* words, *our* languages. Can human language be a fitting vehicle of God's self-revelation? This question dare not deter us. God in grace (could we have survived a more direct means of revelation?) chose to entrust Godself to human language. God risked such revelation to persons who spoke and wrote. In our work as preachers, we must assume this, because trying to avoid this assumption would not be productive.

My concluding unscientific postscript to both a theology of the word and a consideration of preaching is a vision of a miracle. God, in God's self-giving, fills those human words with divine power, "the power of God for salvation to everyone who has faith,…for in [the gospel] the righteousness of God is revealed…" (Rom. 1:16–17). But this miracle is no empty claim; it is shown in its effects, for:

> You have been born anew, not of perishable but of imperishable seed, through the living and enduring word of God. For "All flesh is like grass and all its glory like the flower of grass. The grass withers, and the flower falls, but the word of the Lord endures forever." That word is the good news that was announced to you. (1 Pet. 1:23–25)

2

The Early Church
and the Tradition of Jesus

Over the last century, much interest has centered on the process by which the earliest church developed and passed on the traditions surrounding the figure of Jesus until they were written down in our extant gospels. The discovery of noncanonical gospels in the library at Nag Hammadi in Egypt only increased this interest. The disciplines of *Formgeschichte* and *Redaktionsgeschichte*, as well as the search for sources of the gospels, have focused on those early years.

Since 1960 people involved in the discipline of oral tradition studies have been analyzing systematically the process and results of oral composition and transmission in many different cultures, both ancient and contemporary. The publication in 1960 of Albert Lord's *The Singer of Tales*[1] and subsequently the steady stream of studies of oral composition in both living traditions and ancient artifacts have established this discipline in the arena of academic studies. For a glimpse of the scope and depth of the research, see John Foley, *Oral-Formulaic Theory and Research*.[2] Only recently have the modern methods of oral traditionists been applied to the

---

[1]Albert Bates Lord, *The Singer of Tales* (Cambridge, Mass.: Harvard University Press, 1960).

[2]John Miles Foley, *Oral-Formulaic Theory and Research: An Introduction and Annotated Bibliography* (New York: Garland Publishing, 1985).

biblical documents in order to describe the early process of their transmission through careful study of how oral traditions work in a primarily oral culture.[3]

In this chapter I bring together information from these different disciplines in a way that will help the reader to assess the situation of the early church with reference to oral traditions. A detailed study of the New Testament documents must await later chapters; I present here, rather, a general look at the first-century environment in which the traditions of the earliest Christians were spoken and heard.

First-Century Communication Models

The church began in the matrix of first-century Judaism, which supplied two ready-made communication media. The more obvious of these is the written medium—the Hebrew Scriptures. These documents, which themselves display both obvious and subtle signs of the oral traditions that lie behind them, offered the early followers of Jesus a quiver full of ways to say things. They contain extended narratives, some presented as history, some as saga, some as parables, but all using the long story form to say something important to and about the community that formed them and found its identity in them. They also contain shorter narratives, many embedded in the larger stories and some in other kinds of literature. They include legal codes, some extensive, some brief. There are also chronicles that preserve certain important records without weaving them into an ongoing narrative. There are speeches of the prophets and others; some of these speeches have an eschatological horizon while others are very much rooted in their present. There are wisdom documents, a few carried on a narrative, but many listing, in a rather free way, wise sayings. There are also liturgical texts, including confessions of faith, instructions for cultic activities, prayers, and, of course, psalms.

We must recognize that some of these literary forms are just that, literary forms. The Chronicles, for instance, do not offer much help in terms of oral traditions. The letter of the prophet Jeremiah and the complex writings of Ezekiel[4] are also specifically literary

---

[3]See the survey by Robert Culley, "Oral Tradition and Biblical Studies," in *Oral Tradition* 1/1 (January 1986): 30–65.

[4]See the fascinating study by Ellen F. Davis, *Swallowing the Scroll: Textuality and the Dynamics of Discourse in Ezekiel's Prophecy* (Sheffield, England: Almond Press, 1989).

forms. On the other hand, much of the Hebrew Bible was meant to be recited and thus was composed for the voice and the ear. The longest single chapter of the Bible is Psalm 119, consisting of 176 verses. It is composed as an acrostic, each section of eight verses beginning every verse in the section with the same letter of the Hebrew alphabet so that the twenty-two sections could be kept in order without the help of writing. Also, within each section, nearly every verse (each of which is a doublet) contains at least one term referring to the word of God (law, precept, ordinance, word, promise, etc.). As is true with many other passages of the Hebrew Bible, Psalm 119 is an intricate piece of literature with built-in mnemonic devices to encourage its oral use in the life and worship of Israel.

If the scriptures had offered the totality of the communication palette for the artists of the church, it would have been rich indeed, but also available was a selection of oral colors. Jacob Neusner and others have shown us how difficult it is to state with any assurance the details of rabbinic oral methods before 70 C.E.[5] But at the same time it is obvious that the methods in use at the end of the century were not invented in the trauma of the destruction of Jerusalem. There are hints enough in the Mishnah (c. 200 C.E.) and elsewhere about the pedagogy of the rabbis that we can be sure that they used several methods extensively. They certainly taught in the synagogues and other venues by the method we call midrash, a method of exposition of scripture or of legal questions that had rather firmly set rules of logic, the invention or codification of which is credited to Rabbi Hillel (first century B.C.E.) and a classic example of which comprises Romans 4. They also apparently made a consistent effort to pass on intact the memorable sayings of rabbis from former ages, from time to time adding sayings of their own in mnemonic forms. It is impossible today to judge how close to word-for-word memorization this process was. The rabbis later clearly worked toward exact memorization; but we do know that these sayings were usually connected to a specific sage, and oral tradition studies show an amazing ability by people involved in the process of oral transmission to keep intact the core of the tradition, while giving

---

[5]See Jacob Neusner, "The Rabbinic Traditions about the Pharisees Before 70 A.D.," *Journal of Jewish Studies* 22 (1971): 1–18.

each performance a character stamped by both the performer and the immediate audience.[6]

While it appears that the communication of the first-century scribes was primarily oral (which in itself is a paradox illustrating both the pervasiveness of orality in the first century and our semantic difficulties in dealing with a nonliterate culture), we have the extensive library found at Qumran to attest to the practice of at least the Jewish sectarians who lived there of writing down their own teachings and those of their founder for the sake of posterity. The many genres found there include commentaries, disciplines, and singable poetry, which shows how original orality came to be conserved very quickly through writing, a pattern that was obviously repeated in the development of the New Testament.

In addition to these forms readily available in the Jewish context, the larger environment of the Greco-Roman world offered its own traditions. The rhetoric and poetics codified by Aristotle and others already had a long history in Greece before they were written down. The works of Homer and other poets show us how the ancients could handle extended narratives. The artifacts of the politicians and philosophers indicate a rich selection of ways of presenting data and arguments designed to produce *pistis*. This term, which in the New Testament is usually translated *faith*, was the word Aristotle commonly employed to designate the objective of rhetoric. Appeals to reason and to emotion were included among the techniques used to convince an audience, as can be seen in the example of the Cynic dialectic style called diatribe. Rudolf Bultmann's groundbreaking work on the diatribe-like rhetoric of the apostle Paul in Romans is reported in his published dissertation.[7] Bultmann's identification of the style of writing in Romans with Paul's preaching style stands in need of nuancing, but his research opened the door for scholars to study the effects of Hellenistic rhetoric on the communication of the early church.

There is also evidence that Jews in the diaspora were using a mixture of both Jewish and Hellenistic media to impress their thinking Gentile neighbors with the worship of Yahweh. Both

---

[6]The article by Carol Clover, "The Long Prose Form," *Arkiv for Nordisk Filologi* 101 (1986): 10–39, seems to me to be especially pertinent to students of the Bible, since it deals specifically with nonpoetic forms in a number of different cultures with regard to their fidelity, their creativity, and their positions within a tradition of an extended story.

[7]Rudolf Bultmann, *Der Stil der Paulinischen Predigt und die Kynischstoische Diatribe* (Göttingen: Vandenhoek & Ruprecht, 1910).

Josephus and Philo (contemporaries of the early Christians) used such a mixture with great skill. Philo published many volumes in which he used the Stoic method of allegory to interpret the Hebrew scriptures in the thought forms of his philosophical contemporaries. His predecessors in the Alexandrian Jewish community had translated their scriptures into Greek by 185 B.C.E. This version (the Septuagint) offered a means for Jewish scholars living in various parts of the Roman Empire to introduce interested neighbors to the basic elements of their faith. The success of Christian evangelists among the so-called God-fearers (Acts 10:22, *phoboumenos ton theon*—those who fear God; Acts 17:4, *sebomenon Hellenon*—Hellenists who worship) attests to the effectiveness of this earlier work of *apologia*. Thus, it appears that the environment overflowed with oral and written ways of passing on traditions and convictions, and of doing it both for those within a given community and those outside it.

Jesus as Teacher

In both the New Testament and Josephus, Jesus of Nazareth is referred to as a teacher (*didaskalos*), sometimes using the Hebrew term for teacher, *rabbi*. Several recent studies show indications in the gospels of Jesus' using the pedagogical methods of his time.[8]

Jesus certainly had the powerful personality necessary for keeping the attention of students and casual hearers. Matthew closes his record of the Sermon on the Mount with the report, "the crowds were astounded at his teaching, for he taught them as one having authority, and not as their scribes" (7:28b, 29). Anybody who can meet people busy with labor or commerce and with the simple phrase "Follow me" persuade them to leave their businesses and become his wandering disciples (Mk. 1:16–20 and 2:13–14) is a powerful communicator.

The gospels also show how Jesus used many different forms of communication. Most people are familiar with the parables of Jesus. They followed, to some extent, some of the examples of ancient prophets as well as of rabbis in Palestine, although they

---

[8]The most extensive of these are Birger Gerhardsson, *Memory and Manuscript: Oral Tradition and Written Transmission in Rabbinic Judaism and Early Christianity*, vol. 22, Acta Seminarii Neotestamentici Upsaliensis (Lund: C. K. Gleerup, 1961); Vernon Robbins, *Jesus the Teacher: A Socio-Rhetorical Interpretation of Mark* (Philadelphia: Fortress Press, 1984); and the typically thorough German work of Rainer Riesner, *Jesus als Lehrer: Eine Untersuchung zum Ursprung der Evangelien-Überlieferung* (Tübingen: J. C. B. Mohr, 1988).

are definitely aimed at situations in Jesus' immediate context. The prime example of the parable form is still the story of the prodigal son. Kenneth E. Bailey analyzes what he calls "the literary structure of Luke 15:11–32," a structure that parallels the cyclic or chiastic structure of many texts now recognized as composed orally.[9] His chart of the first half of the story (vv. 11–26) follows:

A There was a man who had two sons	
1 and the younger of them said to his father, "Father, give me the share of the property which falls to me." And he divided his living between them.	A Son Is Lost
2 Not many days later the younger son sold all he had, journeyed into a far country and wasted his property in extravagant living.	Goods Wasted In Expensive living
3 And when he had spent everything a great famine arose in that country and he began to be in want.	Everything Lost
4 So he went and joined himself to one of the citizens of that country and he sent him to his fields to feed pigs.	The Great Sin (Feeding Pigs for gentiles)
5 And he would gladly have eaten the pods which the pigs ate and no one gave him anything.	Total Rejection
6 But when he came to himself he said, "How many of my father's servants have bread to spare but I perish here with hunger.	A Change of Mind
6 "I will arise and go to my father and say to him, 'Father, I have sinned against heaven and before you and am no more worthy to be called your son; make me a servant.'"	An Initial Repentance
5 And he arose and came to his father. And while he was at a great distance his father saw him and had compassion and ran and embraced him and kissed him.	Total Acceptance
4 And the son said to the father, "Father, I have sinned against heaven and before you and am no more worthy to be called your son."	The Great Repentance
3 And the father said to the servants, "Bring the best robe and put it on him and put a ring on his hands and shoes on his feet.	Everything Gained Restored To Sonship
2 And bring the fatted calf and kill it and let us eat and make merry.	Goods Used In Joyful Celebration
1 for this my son was dead and is alive, he was lost and is found." And they began to make merry.	A Son Is Found

A number of Jesus' parables and many other teaching forms end with brief, memorable sayings. Some of these can be found

---

[9]Kenneth E. Bailey, *Poet and Peasant: A Literary Cultural Approach to the Parables in Luke* (Grand Rapids, Mich.: Eerdmans, 1976), 159f.

in similar forms elsewhere; others seem to be peculiar to Jesus. They are poetically crafted with mnemonics, such as parallelisms and rhythm, devices that often remain obvious even in translation. A good example is the parable about coming too late. At the end of that story, Jesus is quoted as saying, "Indeed, some are last who will be first, and some are first who will be last" (Lk. 13:30). The poetic structure is even more obvious in the Greek:

> Kai idou eisin eschatoi hoi esontai protoi,
> Kai eisin protoi hoi esontai eschatoi.

He also took care to show his disciples certain actions as he performed them and to allow them to preach and heal on their own and later to return and discuss the experience (see Luke 9 and 10). It is clear that he was preparing them for leadership, which included various means of communication.

Many of Jesus' teaching opportunities, as recorded in the gospels, were in agonistic (conflict) situations. Although most of the words credited to Jesus are compassionate,[10] his conflicts with a number of individuals and groups in his surroundings (see Lk. 11:37–54) created unforgettable polemic exchanges and ideal situations for applying his teachings to real-life experiences.

Thus, we see that the early church had a tradition that focused on a person who himself had been a teacher and who, therefore, was the source of the tradition. This is shown in the early document 1 Corinthians 11:23, "For I received from the Lord what I also handed on to you." This appears to be a classic statement of oral tradition, a tradition that Paul is now writing down.

The Motives of the Early Church

The early Christians certainly had many models to choose from in their development of oral traditions. They had also a master from whom they had learned and about whom they could speak. But what would motivate them to do such speaking? In the first place, they were convinced that what they had to say was more than an interesting story, more than just one more event of history to narrate, more than a new philosophy from a great teacher. These factors might have been motivation enough to develop a body of tradition, especially since their movement was born within

---

[10]These scenes of confrontation do not include the flitting (negative name-calling) and encomium (extremely positive statements) that Walter Ong identifies with agonistic encounters. See Ong, *Orality and Literacy*, 43–45.

Judaism, with its rich traditions about patriarchs, prophets, and God-chosen rulers. But their conviction was that Jesus was the long-awaited Messiah of God's chosen people. Mark begins his gospel with the heading "The beginning of the good news [*euangeliou*: gospel] of Jesus Christ, the Son of God." They saw him as a divine person, however that divinity was to be described or stated. Their story included, moreover, the resurrection of the crucified Jesus from the grave and his appearances to them. Furthermore, they were convinced that the significance of Jesus was the salvation of the human race. This is not the kind of belief that can remain bottled up in an individual or be kept within the consciousness of a select group of people.

Second, they were apparently commissioned by Jesus himself, after his resurrection, to tell the story. All four gospels and the book of Acts contain some form of a commission. Even though Mark's commission was probably not in the original document, Mark 16:15–18 is a very old addition, in which Jesus tells them to proclaim the gospel to the whole creation. Matthew (28:19–20) emphasizes the teaching function: "make disciples of all nations...and teaching them..." Luke 24:47 has Jesus telling the disciples that "repentance and forgiveness of sins is to be proclaimed (*keruchthenai*) in his name to all nations," while Acts 1:8 quotes Jesus as telling the disciples that they would be his witnesses (*martures*) to the ends of the earth. John places his commission in the closed room just after the resurrection (20:21), when Jesus said, "As the Father has sent me, so I send you." For the purposes of this study, the most interesting of these commission-type statements appears in Matthew 10:27, with a similar parallel in Luke 12:3. Matthew's version reads, "What I say to you in the dark, tell in the light; and what you hear whispered, proclaim (*keruxsate*) from the housetops." Luke's version is more like a prophecy than a commission. But in both cases (since it does not appear in Mark, many scholars assume it was in the lost source of sayings called Q) the emphasis on public speaking is obvious.

Thus, the fact of a commission from Jesus is widely attested, and Matthew connects it specifically with the task of passing on all that Jesus had commanded. The early church was conscious of a commission from the Master, which meant to them a divine commission.

Another conviction that motivated the community of believers was the expectation of the return of the Lord to usher in the judgment day. They did not know how much time was left, so there was a sense of urgency in their getting the word out. It is impossible today to measure the impact on them of eschatology or any other motivation, but it is quite clear that the early church had sufficient reasons to engage in what we call oral transmission of a tradition. Jesus had taught them clearly that the story was to be told (Mk. 14:9) and that the secret was to be shouted from the housetops.

The Time Frame

One of the difficulties of applying the methods and results of oral tradition studies to the documents of the New Testament is the brief span of time between the events being recorded and the writing of the documents. In the case of the Pauline letters the time is as little as fifteen years, and the earliest of the gospels was surely written down, at the latest, not long after 70 C.E., which marks a gap of not more than forty years.[11] This brief period would have allowed the church very little time to develop much that did not come to them directly from the person and events that they were describing. While research into oral traditions indicates how quickly legendary accretions can accumulate around historical figures and events, a few decades is hardly sufficient time to percolate a totally fictional character or to create a nicely polished myth. It would afford the disciples time only to fit their experiences into formats that were familiar in their cultural communication register.

This brief lapse of time also insured that the tradition was developed by and within a community of eyewitnesses. Oral tradition studies have shown how the community of the tradition acts as a check on possible flights of fancy of the bard. Members of an oral community appreciate creative presentations, but they refuse to tolerate changes in the basic story. Such a check would be even more stringent where the community included eyewitnesses of the events and hearers of the words being

---

[11] A number of recognized scholars are once again seriously considering the possibility that all three of the synoptic gospels were written in the form in which we have them before 70 C.E. See J. A. T. Robinson, *Redating the New Testament* (London: SCM, 1976), and Riesner, *Jesus als Lehrer*.

reported. Not only believers but also the opponents of the church were in a position to recognize or to refute the veracity of what was said, thus creating another damper on fictionalizing.

In addition to and connected with these time concerns is the nature of the community of faith itself. It was a community of people for whom the speaking of truth was a primary virtue. The Christian scriptures abound with warnings about control of the tongue (especially Jas. 3:1–12), Jesus taught care in listening (Lk. 8:18), and the rather gruesome story of Ananias and Sapphira (Acts 5:1–11) shows just how serious honesty was, since lying to the church was equivalent to lying to the Holy Spirit.

The Church and Its Media

The church could choose among many ways of conveying its message, ways in use by many different groups in the Roman world. And it used many of them. A brief survey of terminology used in the New Testament reveals the variety of methods, both oral and written. Four terms indicate the scope of modes of oral communication. The two that usually refer to communication within the community, and that are therefore most relevant to the process of passing on the tradition, are *didache* (teaching) and *propheteia* (prophecy). Teaching seems to have been carried on extensively and consistently in all places where the church existed. The position of teacher was highly respected and at times linked with that of pastor (see the lists of gifts and/or ministries in Rom. 12:6–8, 1 Cor. 12:4–31, and Eph. 4:11); in fact, all elders (*episkopoi*) were to be apt to be teachers (*didaktikoi*).

The work of prophecy is not as clear to us from our vantage point. Much research is being done on it at present.[12] It seems clear, however, that certain men and women were recognized as having special abilities to explain scripture or current events or to have insight into future events. The question is being hotly debated as to whether these people spoke words purported to be from the Lord, which were then worked into the narrative framework of the historical Jesus, as has been claimed by many scholars of past generations.[13] Wherever the truth may lie in this regard, it is clear that teachers and prophets were the primary communicators of the tradition to the community of believers.

---

[12]See especially David Hill, *New Testament Prophecy* (Atlanta: John Knox Press, 1979).
[13]Rudolf Bultmann, *The History of the Synoptic Tradition* (New York: Harper & Row, 1963), 40, 134–36.

The other two primary terms referring to oral communication are used mostly with reference to speaking to those outside the community in an attempt to lead them to faith. The terms are *kerugma* (proclamation) and *euangelion* (good news). As is true with teaching and prophecy, verb forms and other nouns are built on the same roots. It has been assumed, perhaps too uncritically, that these two are used, as seems to be true to some extent with *didache* (teaching), to refer primarily to the content of what is said. As a proof text, one often points to 1 Corinthians 1:21, "God decided, through the foolishness of our proclamation, to save those who believe." But I am convinced that *kerugma* points to some extent by its etymology to a manner of presentation and not just to the content of the presentation. The cultural reference of the term is to the work of a king's herald, who repeats in public what has been told him by his king. The herald (*kerux*) would have been taught not only what words to repeat, but also how to communicate them. He did not write them or act them out. He spoke them, loud and clear. What he heard in secret he shouted from wherever he could be heard clearly. Thus, *kerugma* must refer not only to the message, but to the message in the process of being proclaimed—not just to words, but to words preached and heard. So what Paul says in 1 Corinthians 1:21 parallels nicely what he says in Romans 10:17, "Faith comes from what is heard..."

Euangelion, on the other hand, refers to the nature of the message as good news. The part of the tradition that the herald or evangelist would communicate would have been the bare essentials, as is clear in Acts 10:36–43:

> You know the message [God] sent to the people of Israel, preaching peace by Jesus Christ—he is Lord of all. That message spread throughout Judea, beginning in Galilee after the baptism that John announced: how God anointed Jesus of Nazareth with the Holy Spirit and with power; how he went about doing good and healing all who were oppressed by the devil, for God was with him. We are witnesses to all that he did both in Judea and in Jerusalem. They put him to death by hanging him on a tree; but God raised him on the third day and allowed him to appear, not to all the people but to us who were chosen by God as witnesses, and who ate and drank with him after he rose from the dead. He commanded us to preach to the people and to testify that he is the one ordained by God as judge

of the living and the dead. All the prophets testify about him that everyone who believes in him receives forgiveness of sins through his name.

The evangelists presumably presented such a body of information and interpretation in such a way as to bring the hearer to "the obedience of faith" (Rom. 1:5).

In addition to these oral forms, the church soon began to communicate in writing. The letter (*epistole*) was probably the earliest of these written forms, and in the hands of Paul, in much the same way as the letter-essay in the hands of the Greco-Roman scholar, it became a vehicle for conveying both the traditions about Jesus and the application of these to the life of the church. The number of epistles in the New Testament (twenty-one out of twenty-seven documents, and both Acts and Revelation contain letters) testifies to its effectiveness in the early church.

The documents we call gospels use various terms to refer to themselves. The Gospel of Thomas and other similar noncanonical gospels use the term *logioi* to refer to a collection of sayings purporting to go back to Jesus himself. Mark opens with the term *euangelion*, from which we get the designation *gospel* for all of them. Matthew simply uses the term *biblos* (book), as does John (Mt. 1:1; Jn. 20:30). Luke, in his rather complex prologue, uses the term *diegesin* (narrative, report) to describe what others had done and what he intended to do (perhaps even better?). Luke's second volume, the Acts of the Apostles, continues this narrating mode.

The last book of the collection identifies itself as an *apokalupsis* (revelation, literally "uncovering"). One can, of course, identify many other genres of communication embedded in these larger types, but this listing will suffice for our present purposes.

It should be obvious, at least, that the early church had a varied selection of forms at its disposal and that it used many of them in its task of formulating and communicating its word.

Input from Oral Tradition Studies

This survey has sought to show that modern studies of oral traditions can help students of the Christian scriptures better understand the oral background of those scriptures and thereby to better understand both the documents and the nature of the church. Following are five discoveries of oral tradition studies that are of vital interest to the student of communication in early Christianity.

A. Every culture develops and maintains very specific ways of communicating. These include not only the rudiments of that culture's language (vocabulary, syntax, etc.) but also larger forms of speech that signal specific types of communication. For instance, when we hear, "Once upon a time," we know immediately what sort of story we are about to hear, and so we listen in a special way. This complex of communication signals is what scholars of orality call "registers." It is the communication register of the receptor culture that determines the communicability of any given tradition, and therefore this register to a great extent determines the format of the tradition. A study of the New Testament will show how the basic tradition was presented in different ways to different audiences (temple, marketplace, court; Jerusalem, Asia, Greece, Rome, etc.).

B. Generally speaking, extended narratives are not unusual in oral traditions. They are passed on with great fidelity to the core story, but rarely with word-for-word memorization. It is now being argued[14] that the two-source hypothesis of the writing of the synoptics should be reviewed in the light of such studies, that is, that the differences and similarities among the gospels can be accounted for by independent oral traditions and that the basic presuppositions of form criticism must be reevaluated.[15]

C. Briefer statements are often passed on via word-for-word or nearly word-for-word memorization. This is especially to be noted with aphoristic statements, songs or ballads, and ritualized speech.

D. In primarily oral cultures, the society itself (or a subgroup of it) acts as the preserver or guarantor of the tradition. This is especially interesting in light of the willingness of the early Christians to suffer and die for the sake of their message.

E. Historical accuracy does not depend on dispassionate research and reporting. In fact, the historian can find

---

[14]See Riesner, *Jesus als Lehrer.*
[15]See Ben F. Meyer, *Jesus and the Oral Gospel Tradition* (Sheffield, England: JSOT Press, 1991); 424–40; and Peter Stuhlmacher, in *The Gospel and the Gospels* (Grand Rapids, Mich.: Eerdmans, 1991), 1–25.

trustworthy accounts in traditions that have only a minor interest in historicity, since the information they pass on often tends to be accurate when they have no reason for falsifying it.[16] Thus, perhaps Christian scholarship has been too reticent to make historical claims on the basis of its documents and their oral precursors.

Conclusion

In order to apply the discoveries of orality studies to the analysis of the gospels, we must undergo a paradigm shift, adjusting some of the presuppositions and questions of contemporary biblical scholarship in several directions. For instance, we should certainly suspend the assumption that every word that Jesus spoke was unique. It seems much more in tune with normal communication practices to assume that Jesus himself would have told some of his stories several times, adapting them to his audiences and his purposes. According to orality research, we should expect that his aphorisms (concise, poetic sayings) would have been crystallized early, while the narrative meshalim (parables, etc.) would have been much more flexible. Given that example, it should not be difficult to imagine his followers doing the same with their stories about him. It is important for us to remember that for both Jesus and the early church oral communication was the primary medium. As Richard Ward has put it:

> While the majority of those in the Christian movement preferred orality as its repository for sacred stories, its leaders freely employed the art of writing. Texts were designed to capture the distinct features of oral discourse and encode them into written signs. In Christian worship, texts were returned to oral space by way of the public reader.[17]

---

[16]Jan Vansina, *Oral Tradition as History* (Madison: University of Wisconsin Press, 1985).

[17]Richard Ward, *Speaking from the Heart: Preaching with Passion* (Nashville: Abingdon Press, 1992), 49. He underscores the continuation of this practice into the second century by citing Justin Martyr's oft-quoted lines, "On the day called after the sun a meeting of all who live in cities or in the country takes place at a common spot and the Memoirs of the Apostles or the writings of the Prophets are read as long as time allows. When the reader is finished the leader delivers an address through which he exhorts and requires them to follow noble teaching and examples" (Justin Martyr, 67).

Since when we are dealing with the documents of the New Testament we are dealing with a repository of oral communication, perhaps we should follow the lead of scholars of orality and drop the search for "originals." In orality studies there is no such thing as an original, since every performance of an oral tradition is heard as an original, even in cases where the story is well known by the audience.[18] The tradition is the property (and to a great extent, the product) of a community, and to make a historical search for the original makes no sense in such a context.

It appears that the intersection of the disciplines of orality studies and biblical studies will enrich both and will prove to be exceptionally beneficial to women and men who are committed to preaching (oral communication) the message conveyed by the Christian scriptures (all of which in one way or another have roots in orality). In the next three chapters we shall look more closely at that intersection with regard to a gospel, to the book of Acts, and to the epistles of the New Testament, keeping in mind that we are interested not only in the history behind ancient documents, but also in contemporary preaching.

---

[18]Lord, *Singer of Tales*, 100f. Lord concludes his discussion of this phenomenon by writing, "In a sense each performance is 'an' original, if not 'the' original."

3

Oral Characteristics
of the Gospel of Luke

Introduction

The statement of the gospel by the apostle Paul in 1 Corinthians 15:3–8 seems to most of us a natural way of saying what God has accomplished in Jesus Christ. Paul gets right to the heart of the matter and outlines the facts and their interpretation, listing a number of witnesses to the resurrection of Jesus to close the description.

> For I handed on to you as of first importance what I in turn had received: that Christ died for our sins in accordance with the scriptures, and that he was buried, and that he was raised on the third day in accordance with the scriptures, and that he appeared to Cephas, then to the twelve. Then he appeared to more than five hundred brothers and sisters at one time, most of whom are still alive, though some have died. Then he appeared to James, then to all the apostles. Last of all, as to one untimely born, he appeared to me.

On the other hand, we have trouble relating many of the stories of the canonical gospels to our patterns of thought. Announcements by angels, miracles, cosmic portents, divine voices, graves opening, and so on, do not appear in modern books, except in those branded as fantasy.

What we have here is a classic clash of ways of dealing with information—differing communication styles. To people thinking in a certain way (Aristotelian rhetoric, essay form), 1 Corinthians 15:3–11 is a straightforward statement of facts. Actually, "straightforward" describes well what many call linear thinking. On the other hand, to people with an oral tradition mode of thinking (and these same people could be linear thinkers in a different frame of mind), it would seem utterly disrespectful to tell the story of Jesus in the dry, "just the facts, please," style of our newspapers and many biographies. Hero stories were always spoken in certain forms, using traditional speech formulas and scenes of life transition; and telling Jesus' story without those traditional forms would have seemed to dishonor him and distort the impression he made on other people.

In fact, even Paul connected his highly developed christology to several of the major patterns of thinking of his day: wisdom theology (1 Cor. 1:18—2:16), apocalyptic (2 Thess. 2:1–12), rabbinic midrash (Rom. 4), prophecy (Rom. 9—11), allegory (Gal. 4:21–31), and Hellenistic rhetoric (note the structure of the argument of Philemon), to name just the most obvious.

We should not, then, be surprised to find characteristics of oral traditional communication in the New Testament, nor should such findings threaten our acceptance of the authority of scripture. On the contrary, were we to discover a document purporting to come from a primarily oral culture that did not display such marks, we should be immediately suspicious of forgery.

In fact, the very statement of the gospel in logical, historical terms in 1 Corinthians 15 begins with a typical statement of the process of oral tradition ("I handed on to you...what I in turn had received"). The historical credibility of the New Testament is supported by the many signs of its direct lineage from Jesus via the path of oral tradition and its dependence on various patterns of first-century thinking.

In addition, if, as ancient tradition has it,[1] the gospels are basically accounts in writing of the preaching (oral transmission) of the early church, and if Paul and the other "writers" (they appear to have dictated most of their works to amanuenses) of the rest of the New Testament documents were first and foremost

---

[1]See Eusebius, *Ecclesiastical History* II, xv–xvi, and III, xxiv.

preachers, we should expect to find signs of orality in the gospels and Acts and references to orality throughout the New Testament.

These next chapters, then, comprise a brief survey of several New Testament documents, pointing out characteristic marks of orality in them. Since others have done such work on Mark and Matthew,[2] and since this chapter cannot pretend to accomplish more than a superficial examination, I limit my survey of the gospels to Luke, then in the next two chapters discuss some obvious features in Acts and examine some important statements in the epistles.

The Format of Luke's Gospel

Since Luke gives us a formal prologue to his gospel, it is important to see how he describes his intent and method. In Luke 1:1–4 he indicates first of all his awareness that others (many: *polloi*) have contributed to compiling a narrative (*diegesin*) about the events that had taken place among them, as those reports were handed down (*paredosan*, the typical term for oral tradition) by those who were, from the beginning, eyewitnesses and servants of the word. To this point we see Luke referring to his acquaintance with both oral and written reports of the things he intends to write about. He then briefly describes the process and intent of the preparation of his document. He claims to have given careful attention (*parekolouthekoti*, a word that likely refers to research or investigation) to everything from early on, thus highlighting the care he has given to his preparation.[3] He then describes his writing as being done accurately (*akribos*) and in sequence (*kathexes*) so that Theophilus may have thorough knowledge (*epignos*) of the reliability (*asphaleian*) of the instruction he had received (presumably through oral teaching). Thus, it is clear that Luke is setting out to do more than to record what he is hearing or even reading. He is composing a literary document that finds sources of its content in both oral and written traditions. Therefore, if we can identify marks of oral composition in Luke, there can be little doubt of the importance of oral tradition in the early church.

---

[2]Werner H. Kelber, *The Oral and the Written Gospel: The Hermeneutics of Speaking and Writing in the Synoptic Tradition, Mark, Paul, and Q* (Philadelphia: Fortress Press, 1983), and Charles Lohr, "Oral Techniques in the Gospel of Matthew," *Catholic Biblical Quarterly* 23 (1961): 403–35. See also several essays in Wansbrough, *Jesus and the Oral Gospel Tradition*.

[3]See Joseph A. Fitzmyer, *The Gospel According to Luke I–IX*, Anchor Bible (Garden City, N.Y.: Doubleday, 1981).

Scholars have often overlooked the reliance of the early Christians on oral delivery as the primary and most trustworthy medium of communication. Even Calvin betrays his bias toward literature when he summarizes Luke's prologue, "In short, Luke's meaning is this: 'that, since thou now hast those things committed faithfully to writing which thou hadst formerly learned by oral statements, thou mayest place a stronger reliance on the received doctrine.'"[4] But as suggested earlier, if we can put aside our bias toward writing, we should be able to recognize the power that the early Christians recognized in both the spoken word of Jesus and the preaching of their contemporaries about Jesus.

Signs of Orality in Luke

The two most basic and characteristic marks of orally composed narratives or poetry, according to Lord, are repeating formulas and themes, which became the expected vehicles by which information was communicated.[5] Formulas, in this sense, are words and phrases used repetitively by the speaker as memory aids for both speaker and audience. Some of these formulas seem to have been in general use in the culture or a smaller group, while others are peculiar to the individual speaker (idiolectic). Themes, on the other hand, are frameworks in which certain types of narrative were customarily related. Werner Kelber has given to the field of New Testament studies a grid of four themes, which he illustrates from Mark's gospel;[6] and Henry J. Cadbury has summarized nicely for us oral formulas in Luke and Acts, which he identifies as Luke's peculiar literary style.[7]

Themes

The following brief overview of Luke's gospel seeks out the kinds of narrative structures that orality scholars identify as themes. In literature based on oral communication one expects to find rather rigid frameworks in which similar kinds of stories are told. Such repetition signals orality, since literary thinkers attempt to omit what they perceive as redundancies. Literacy prizes creativity, while orality depends on mnemonic structures that are

---

[4]John Calvin, *Commentary on a Harmony of the Evangelists, Matthew, Mark, and Luke*, reprinted in *Calvin's Commentaries* (Grand Rapids, Mich.: Baker Books, 1981), 6.

[5]Lord, *Singer of Tales*, 30–98.

[6]Kelber, *The Oral and the Written Gospel*, 44–64.

[7]Henry J. Cadbury, "Four Features of Lukan Style," in *Studies in Luke–Acts*, ed. Leander E. Keck and Louis Martyn (London: SPCK, 1976), 87–102.

familiar to all hearers. What follows, then, is a brief analysis of oral narrative themes in Luke.

Heroic Stories

These are accounts of miracles, either performed by Jesus or involved with his birth (we'll pass over the resurrection until chapter 5). Kelber offers the following outline as characteristic:[8]

  I. Exposition of Healing
     a. arrival of healer and sick person
     b. staging of public forum (onlookers)
     c. explication of sickness
     d. request for help
     e. public scorn or skepticism

  II. Performance of Healing
     a. utterance of healing formula
     b. healing gestures
     c. statement of cure

  III. Confirmation of Healing
     a. admiration/confirmation formula
     b. dismissal of healed person
     c. injunction of secrecy
     d. propagation of healer's fame

As many have recognized, IIIc. is a special characteristic of Mark, which we won't expect to find as often in Luke. But the others, as we shall see, appear often enough to be recognized as a thematic pattern.

MIRACLES SURROUNDING THE NATIVITY: **1:5—2:38.** These are, of course, not healing miracles, but they placard the special birth of Jesus, distinguishing him as a person sent by the Divinity with a special mission. The special birth of John (later to be called "the Baptizer") connects Jesus with his forerunner, while the miraculous events surrounding Mary's conceiving and the angelic messengers contrast nicely with the very human suspense of a long trip and a full inn. Luke (or the oral reporter from whom he got the stories) connects Jesus from the first with the poor and marginalized people in his culture, especially as he pictures the angelic announcement to shepherds, those ever suspect and ritually unclean characters who are the first to visit Jesus in his extremely humble birthplace.

---

[8]Kelber, *The Oral and the Written Gospel*, 46.

PRECOCIOUS CHILDHOOD: 2:41–51. Luke is the only canonical gospel that deals with the boyhood of Jesus, although some rather fantastic stories of his childhood appear in some noncanonical documents.[9] Luke focuses on one event, usually understood as equivalent to Jesus' bar mitzvah, when he mystified the scholars in the temple with his great wisdom. This brief glimpse of the boy growing into manhood prepares the reader/listener for Jesus the teacher and healer.

HEALINGS. Note how Kelber's outline appears very consistently in the eleven healing stories Luke offers his readers.

4:31–41: Here a demon-possessed person is in the synagogue in Capernaum, where Jesus faces him. The cry for help in this instance (because of the demon) is a cry against Jesus and his power. The healing is done when Jesus rebukes the demon; Luke notes that no harm was done by the demon as he left the man, that the crowd was amazed, and that the fame of Jesus spread.

5:12–16: Jesus is in an unnamed city, where a man with leprosy approaches him and asks for healing. Jesus touches him and speaks to him. He tells the man to present himself to the priests to confirm the healing, and again the fame of Jesus spreads.

5:17–26: In this familiar account, Jesus is teaching in a very crowded house when four people lower a paralytic friend from the roof into the space in front of Jesus. He notes their faith and forgives the man's sins. In response to the negative reaction of the Pharisees, Jesus commands the man to rise and walk, which he does. Great amazement is reported in the crowd.

6:6–11: Once again Jesus is teaching in a synagogue on the sabbath day when he becomes conscious of a man present with a withered hand. In spite of the scribes and Pharisees present, who are watching to catch him in an error, he heals the man, leaving his enemies furious.

7:1–10: Some Jewish elders in Capernaum appeal to Jesus on behalf of a Roman centurion whose slave is ill. Jesus and the centurion converse about the nature of authority, and Jesus (according to the man's faith) heals the slave from a distance.

7:11–17: Jesus goes to Nain with a crowd of his followers and encounters a funeral procession, which he stops. He then raises the son of the widow, and his fame spreads once again.

---

[9]See especially the Infancy Gospel of Thomas.

8:40–42, 49–56: This is one of a pair of healings reported together, which makes it and its partner unique. The structure, however, is present anyway. There is a crowd, and Jairus' daughter is dying. Jairus begs Jesus to come and heal her, when they are interrupted by the other healing. Eventually word comes that the girl has died, but Jesus goes and raises her. Here he instructs the household to keep the whole episode secret. This is the only instance where Luke uses the secrecy motif, so important in Mark. Luke appears to follow the parallel story in Mark 5:43, although Luke's wording is radically different from Mark's.

8:43–48: This healing, which is placed within the structure of the one above, is of the woman with the long-term hemorrhage. She touches the fringe of Jesus' clothes and is healed. He senses it and explains to her that her faith accomplished it.

13:10–17: Here we have another confrontation in a synagogue on the Sabbath. Jesus sees a woman possessed by a spirit that had crippled her for eighteen years. He calls out to her and lays hands on her, healing her, whereupon she praises God. The synagogue leader starts a controversy over this breaking of sabbath regulations.

17:11–19: This story takes place in the boundary land between Samaria and Galilee, where ten lepers approach Jesus and ask for healing. He commands them to go to the priests; they do so and are healed on the way. One (a Samaritan) returns to thank Jesus.

18:35–43: This last healing interrupts Jesus' final journey to Jerusalem. He is accosted in Jericho, by a blind man who requests healing. Jesus heals him with a word, and there is great rejoicing.

Luke's story pattern in these instances differs only slightly from Mark's. In none of his miracle stories does Luke record public scorn or skepticism, although in several he mentions scribes and Pharisees who are trying to catch Jesus breaking a law. There is almost always a crowd present, but not always a public conversation. Luke seems to be interested primarily in the compassion of Jesus and the spreading of that reputation. However, with the exception of Ie. and IIIc. in Kelber's pattern (and IIIc. appears in 8:56), Luke's healing miracle reports follow the same sequence as do Mark's.

NATURE MIRACLES: 5:1–11; 8:22–25; 9:10–17. The first two of these three miracles take place on the sea (the miraculous catch of fish and the stilling of the storm), and both of them are told from the standpoint of the deep impression they left on the disciples. The third is the feeding of the five thousand, and Luke records no response at all to this miracle; although the very next pericope is Peter's confession of Jesus as Messiah. So Luke's nature miracles seem to be for the sake of the disciples and not for that of unbelievers.

TRANSFIGURATION: **9:28–36.** Here too we have an experience permitted for only three of the disciples. The miracle itself, of course, points clearly to the special role Jesus was playing in the drama of God's plan of salvation, since he is pictured as consulting with Moses and Elijah and as being singled out by the heavenly voice as the one to heed. This heroic theme pattern had been set in Jewish tradition in the accounts of the mountaintop theophanies to Moses in Exodus 3:1–6 and to Elijah in 1 Kings 19:8–18, so their presence here marks Jesus as being in their lineage and yet their superior.

Polarization Stories

These are special miracles that illustrate the conflict between Jesus and the cosmic powers of evil. They are usually exorcisms, but the account of Jesus' temptation might also fit here. The exaggeration of these stories is characteristic of oral tradition, in which opposing sides are generally and clearly portrayed as good or evil. There is very little "gray area" (ambiguity) in public communication within a primarily oral culture, in contrast to later literary conventions.[10]

TEMPTATION IN THE WILDERNESS: **4:1–13.** This narrative makes it clear at the beginning of the ministry of Jesus that his conflict is actually with the cosmic power of evil and not just with misguided mortals. Among other things that this story accomplishes, it makes clear that Jesus has the ability to withstand and defeat demonic power.

THE GERASENE DEMONIAC: **8:26–39.** This confrontation with evil powers inhabiting a human being displays the demons' recognition of the person and power of Jesus and his control over them.

9:37–43: The story of the epileptic boy whom the disciples could not help highlights the special place and power of Jesus in this cosmic battle.

---

[10]Ong, *Interfaces of the Word,* 108.

11:37–54: The conflict with the Pharisees is told in terms that nearly match these other accounts. In retrospect, as the story would have been heard, this confrontation is seen as part of the cosmic conflict.

Didactic Stories

Sometimes referred to as "apophthegms,"[11] these stories show Jesus in conflict with an individual or group and end in a memorable saying of Jesus. Such memorable sayings offer a clear signal of a teacher in an oral culture expressing a thought poetically so that the hearers can easily remember the exact saying.[12]

5:29–39: A banquet at Levi's house with tax collectors offers an occasion for the Pharisees to complain about Jesus' eating with sinners. Jesus replies, "Those who are well have no need of a physician, but thos who are sick; I have come to call not the righteous but sinners to repentance." Whereupon, they ask him why his disciples do not fast as do John's disciples; and he replies with the metaphor of the wedding and bridegroom. Luke follows up with the parables of the new cloth patching an old garment and of the new wine and old wineskins.

6:1–5: The disciples pluck and eat some grain on the Sabbath, which causes some Pharisees to criticize them. Jesus reminds them of David's eating the bread of the Presence, and then says, "The Son of Man is lord of the sabbath."

7:36–50: While eating in the home of a Pharisee, Jesus is approached by a sinful woman, who anoints his feet with oil and tears and dries them with her hair. Simon, the Pharisee, interprets this event as a sign that Jesus is not a prophet, since a godly man would not have permitted such a woman to touch him. Jesus then tells the parable of the creditor who cancels a large debt and a small one, explaining "the one to whom little is forgiven, loves little."

9:49–50: This very brief pericope shows John the disciple telling Jesus that they had tried to stop somebody from casting out demons in the name of Jesus; but Jesus says, "whoever is not against you is for you."

---

[11]The word stems from the Greek *apophthengamai*, meaning to declare or address, usually as an inspired utterance. See any lexicon of first-century Greek.

[12]See the very helpful treatment of the traditional *shema* of the Jewish teacher in Birger Gerhardsson, *The Origins of the Gospel Traditions* (Philadelphia: Fortress Press, 1979), 67–77. See also Friedrich Hauck, "Parable," in Gerhard Friedrich and Gerhard Kittel, eds., *Theological Dictionary of the New Testament*, vol. 5 (Grand Rapids, Mich.: Eerdmans, 1979), 747–51.

18:18–30: The familiar story of the rich young ruler sets the stage for a series of teachings: "It is easier for a camel to go through the eye of a needle than for someone who is rich to enter the kingdom of God." "What is impossible for mortals is possible for God." "There is no one who has left house or wife or brothers or parents or children, for the sake of the kingdom of God, who will not get back very much more in this age, and in the age to come eternal life."

These didactic stories show fine variety, some of them being very simple, while others comprise a whole series of teachings imbedded in a narrative. The final one is a good example of how flexible people could be with the story, while recalling precisely the heart of the teaching. The details differ somewhat in the three synoptic gospels, but the three didactic statements listed above are nearly word-for-word the same. The only exception is the third, for which both Matthew and Mark give more details.

So far we have been looking at stories *about* Jesus. Before turning to stories from the lips of Jesus, we should summarize our findings to this point. The stories that focus on the conception, birth, and upbringing of Jesus are similar to birth and infancy narratives in many heroic epics from a number of ancient cultures. The details differ widely, but the reports of seemingly miraculous aspects of the hero's birth and childhood are quite common.[13]

As we noted, the structure of healing narratives in Luke is nearly identical to that in Mark, which indicates a dominant pattern for such stories in early Christianity. This is precisely what Albert Lord and other scholars of orality have christened a "theme."[14] At the same time, we see in 8:40ff. the creativity of putting one of these stories inside another. Since the two stories are thus intertwined in all three synoptic gospels, we can either credit Mark with the structure and see Matthew and Luke copying from Mark (in this case Mark gives more detail than either of the others), or we can assume that the oral reports of these activities were all similar and are thus historically trustworthy. In either case, we are working with an assumption that cannot at this time be proved or disproved.

In Luke, the polarization stories come closest to what is called agonistic (conflict) narrative. In many traditional stories one finds

---

[13]These are helpfully collected in David R. Cartlidge and David L. Dungan, *Documents for the Study of the Gospels* (Philadelphia: Fortress Press, 1980), 119–36.

[14]Lord, *Singer of Tales*, 68–98.

much flitting (name-calling and personal challenges to an enemy). A good example is the story of David and Goliath, in 1 Samuel 17. According to verse 42, the giant "disdained" David, which led to his "dissing" the boy, to use the vernacular of American streets. "The Philistine said to David, 'Am I a dog, that you come to me with sticks?' And the Philistine cursed David by his gods. The Philistine said to David, 'Come to me, and I will give your flesh to the birds of the air and to the wild animals of the field.'" David eventually replied, "This very day the LORD will deliver you into my hand, and I will strike you down and cut off your head; and I will give the dead bodies of the Philistine army this very day to the birds of the air and to the wild animals of the earth, so that all the earth may know that there is a God in Israel" (vv. 43–46). Because of our very literate approach to Jesus, such behavior seems not to fit comfortably in our understanding of his life, but the gospels show him in direct conflict with individuals, groups, Satan, and demons.

Finally, the didactic stories mentioned above are good examples of a type one finds regularly in stories from traditionally oral societies concerning a wise hero. Wisdom literature generally connects wise sayings (proverbs, etc.) with application in life, so the most vivid way to present the saying is to imbed it in a narrative. The five examples of didactic stories given in Luke follow a pattern closely enough to be identified as themes. The stories that Luke records about Jesus are clearly the type of story told in oral tradition situations. Having looked at Luke's stories about Jesus, we can turn now to stories recorded as told by Jesus himself.

Parabolic Stories

These are stories from the mouth of Jesus, what Gerhardsson has helpfully labeled "narrative meshalim."[15] They have no set structure, but they reflect realistically a slice of life, with a memorable twist toward the end. It should prove helpful to categorize the parables by style, although for our purposes extensive commentary on the individual passages is unnecessary.

Luke includes more of these stories than do either of the other two synoptists. This is not surprising, since Luke has more stories

---

[15]Birger Gerhardsson, "The Narrative Meshalim in the Synoptic Gospels," *New Testament Studies* 34 (1988): 339–63.

peculiar to him. In the following list we shall refer to the synoptic parallel passages when there are such.[16]

BRIEF METAPHORICAL SAYINGS. These short sayings illustrate the use an effective oral communicator can make of familiar visual experiences of the hearers.

6:39–45: A series of brief parables (Mt. 7:3–5). As part of an extended teaching, Jesus refers to blind guides, to judgmentalism in terms of seeing the speck in another's eye, and to the good tree bearing good fruit.

12:24–28: Birds and flowers (Mt. 6:26–30). Here we have the familiar reference to birds (ravens) and flowers (lilies) taken care of by God.

13:20–21: Yeast (Mt. 13:33). The woman here needs but a little yeast to leaven three measures of flour.

BRIEF STORY FORMS. Here we find narratives told with very few details. Just enough description is offered to permit the hearers to identify with some aspect of the story.

5:37–39: Wine/wineskins (Mt. 9:17, Mk. 2:22). There is no plot to this story, just the use of the metaphor that came to determine much of the self-understanding of the early church, as witnessed to by its appearance in all three synoptics. The early Christians were doing a new thing, so they became bold to do it in new ways.

6:47–49: Wise and foolish builders (Mt. 7:24–27). Again we find a story told with few details of the plot. The wise builder's house withstands the storms, and the foolish builder's house does not. As the story stands in the gospels, the hearer must supply the details.

8:16–18: Lamp/lampstand (Mt. 5:15, Mk. 4:21–22). Again we have a threefold tradition, indicating its great importance in the development of the identity of the early church. Followers of Jesus are to be lights, on display for all the world to see.

11:33–36: Lamp again (Mt. 6:22–23). The lamp metaphor is now directed inward, with the warning that the disciples should see to it that the whole life is characterized by light.

12:35–40: Wedding and thief in the night (Mt. 25:8–13; 24:42–44). Matthew's version of these stories is more detailed than is Luke's. In Luke we have just the bare outlines of plots,

---

[16]Gerhardsson, "The Narrative Meshalim," 39–63, lists and classifies the parables differently than I do (334), but analyzes them in comparison to similar texts in the Old Testament in a very helpful way.

emphasizing the importance of being prepared for the absence or coming at an unannounced time of the Son of man.

13:6–9: Fig tree. This story is told with a bit more detail than the ones mentioned above. It even contains dialogue. However, it is still relatively brief, casting the spotlight on fruit bearing as the sign of health.

13:18–19: Mustard seed (Mt. 13:31–32, Mk. 4:30–32). This brief kingdom parable emphasizes surprising growth.

EXTENDED STORIES. In these masterfully crafted longer narratives Jesus holds his hearers in a familiar experience only to surprise or shock them with a twist toward the end.

8:4–15: Sower (Mt. 13:1–9, Mk. 4:1–9). Here we find not only a nicely crafted story, but also an interpretation of it. We usually refer to this as the parable of the sower, but the emphasis seems to be on the variety of soils that receive the seed in a variety of ways. The story makes it clear that the task of communicating the gospel ("The seed is the word of God," v. 11) is not an easy one, but that it will have surprisingly positive results.

10:25–37: Good Samaritan. In its first-century Near Eastern context, this beautiful little tale would have been shocking. For a Jew to make a Samaritan the hero of a story would certainly have drawn the hearer's attention to the fact that relationships are to be built on acts of compassion, not on bloodlines.

12:16–21: Rich farmer. This parable invites the hearer to put life's various issues in the perspective of eternity. It is a narrative way of saying, "You can't take it with you."

12:41–48: Prudent slave (Mt. 24:45–51). Jesus tells this story to answer Peter's question about the application of the brief version of the thief in the night parable. The prudent slave is the one whose master will find working when he returns unexpectedly.

13:24–30: Coming too late. This parable serves as a warning to those who want to postpose a decision to enter the reign of God.

14:16–24: Banquet (Mt. 22:1–10). This story also warns hearers to act on the invitation to God's banquet when the opportunity comes. Otherwise some surprising people will be brought in before them.

15:3–7: The lost sheep (Mt. 18:12–14). This first of the series of the lost stories emphasizes the importance of the individual sheep to the shepherd.

15:8–10: The lost coin. This parable puts the lost item at home and describes the woman's diligence in searching for it.

15:11–32: The prodigal son. This story is longer and much more detailed than the other two. It seems to have two endings and thus two issues to deal with. The first is the surprising grace of the father, who forgets his powerful position and runs down the road to greet the returning son. The second is the warning against those, however righteous they may be, who, like the older brother, refuse reconciliation and are left out of the celebration. In all three of these parables, celebration is a major theme, and one should not miss the party.

16:1–9: The steward. Again we find Jesus commending a character who is less than righteous. This steward was dishonest, but his wise (crafty?) actions in collecting a percentage of debts owed his master are commended. Jesus' followers are encouraged to have not only a heavenly vision, but also some wordly common sense.

16:19–31: The rich man and Lazarus. There are many levels of meaning in this parable about the rich man and the beggar, who both die. On one level it exhibits the attitude that riches tend to encourage, that the rich person deserves to be served. Even in Hades, the rich man expected the beggar to come from heaven to help him, and failing that, to go from heaven to help his family.

18:1–8: The judge. This story is an audacious comparison of a godless judge and the God he rejected. The judge helps the widow in order to get rid of her. God will "grant justice to his chosen ones who cry to him day and night" (v. 7).

18:9–14: The Pharisee and the publican. Here is another shocker. The publican (tax collector) rather than the Pharisee is righteous, indicating that humble repentance rather than public works leads to righteousness.

19:11–27: Talents (Mt. 25:14–30). Here is another story about an absent master and servants' behavior in his absence. The servant punished in this story has not done anything unethical. He simply has not done anything. He hid what he was entrusted with so as not to lose it; so when the master came, the servant lost what he had hidden.

Many excellent publications are available that deal with the nature of narrative in general and parables in particular, most of which indicate the nature of the oral communication of Jesus in his culture. Even a superficial acquaintance with rabbinic literature shows how extensive such narrative thinking was in first-century Judaism. Jesus was certainly a master storyteller who could draw his hearers into the fabric of a narrative, only to shock them with an unexpected turn toward the end. His use of parables as a primary medium of teaching is not only not surprising, but for one familiar with communication in primarily oral cultures, the absence of such narratives would call into question the historical veracity of the written records.

It seems to me that in nearly all recent literature on parables a very important point is missed. So much attention is given to what a parable meant or means that one rarely finds the question, What did it do? For the storyteller even today, the "point" of a story is of secondary importance. Primary is the effect, the function, of the story. I contend that Jesus, the master storyteller, told stories to draw hearers into an experience of the reality of the reign of God that no syllogism or proposition could offer. If we are to understand how these narrative meshalim were heard in a primarily oral setting, we need to put ourselves into the story instead of just analyzing it objectively.

Other Categories of Themes

Two other kinds of information deserve our attention.

THE GENEALOGY OF JESUS: 3:23–38. It seems to the literate mind both cumbersome and unnecessary for families to memorize genealogies; but this practice is still quite common in oral cultures. Luke's listing begins with Jesus and progresses back, so it lists people as "son of…" back to "Adam, son of God"; whereas Matthew (1:2ff.) begins with Abraham and lists people who begat descendants. Either way we have neatly categorized lists, with rhythmic repetitions to aid memorization. First-century culture determined the importance of lineage; oral communication determined the mnemonic form.

ACCOUNTS OF JESUS' TEACHING AND PREACHING: 4:14–32. Jesus announces his own ministry when, in the synagogue in Nazareth, he reads Isaiah 61:1–2 and says, "Today this scripture has been fulfilled in your hearing." In this Isaiah text appear the two verbs that, as we saw in chapter 2, become most characteristic in describing the preaching of Jesus and of the early church: *euangelizo* (preach good news) and *kerusso* (proclaim).

4:42–44: Here the two verbs introduced in the previous passage are applied to the work of Jesus. He breaks away from his healing activity in Capernaum with the explanation, *euangelisasthai me dei* ("I must proclaim the good news"). Luke follows this with the editorial comment, *Kai en kerusson* ("and so he continued proclaiming").

6:17–49: Luke's Sermon on the Plain, which parallels much of Matthew's Sermon on the Mount, is an example of extended teaching, covering several issues and using several communication styles, including parables, metaphors, aphorisms, and direct explanation and exhortation.

8:1–3: This summary, which is characteristic of a number of editorial summaries in both Luke and Acts, characterizes Jesus' ministry of the word as *kerusson kai euangelizomenos ten basileian tou theou* ("proclaiming and bringing the good news of the kingdom of God").

8:39: Jesus sends the healed demoniac to narrate (*diegou*) what God had done for him, and Luke tells us that he went away proclaiming (*kerusson*).

9:2, 6: Jesus commissioned the Twelve to proclaim (*kerussein*) the kingdom, and Luke tells us that they preached the good news (*euangelizomenoi*).

9:18–27: Here we see Jesus teaching the Twelve by using questions and answers, metaphors, and direct speech.

11:1–13: Jesus teaches his disciples about prayer by first giving them a model of prayer and then telling a parable that illustrates the importance of persistence in prayer.

12:1—13:35: In these two chapters, Luke has collected teachings of Jesus given in a number of different places and to various audiences. We see him on these occasions using the same variety of forms that we have noted earlier.

We have seen a formidable number of themes in the gospel of Luke. This same list has been interpreted as pieces of the redactional work of the editor or editors of the gospel. It should be recognized that a scholar involved in orality studies would see the list as evidence of the living oral communication of the community that lived by and passed on the information. In other words, the presence of these themes indicates that the writer was either recording oral traditions as he received them or writing in that oral style.

Formulas

We turn now to a consideration of the other primary characteristics of orality, oral formulas in Luke's gospel. Cadbury sees what I am calling oral formulas as literary stylistic devices. However, he does call at least one of Luke's tendencies "Homeric."[17] He goes on to write:

> It may be worthwhile to mention two other elements in the literary methods to which Luke was heir, that would increase his skill with synonymous paraphrase. One is the habit of combining synonyms in pairs which he shares with the Greek writers; the other is the Jewish habit of *parallelismus membrorum.*
>
> As for the former, certain combinations in Luke–Acts are standard Greek cliches, while others apparently chosen by him are created ad hoc much as is done in other languages or writers.[18]

When Cadbury wrote this in 1966, he appears not to have been aware that this description of Luke's "literary style" is a rather good description of characteristics of oral performance and/or production. Let us examine several of these characteristics as marks of orality.

Much of what Cadbury labels "repetition" orality scholars call formula.[19] These include single words and also several words linked as phrases or descriptive statements. Here are merely a few of the more obvious instances:

1:32/35: Here Luke connects the angels' song with Old Testament prophecy through the use of repetition of "Son of the Most High," "Son of God," and "the Most High."

1:57/2:6: In these passages the term *tou tekein auten* (time "for [her] to give birth" is translated in various ways) is used in the narratives of the births of both John and Jesus.

2:18/33: Here the verb *thaumazo* (be amazed) is used to describe the reaction of Mary and Joseph to Jesus' birth and to the surrounding events after both the visit by the shepherds and the later events in the temple.

9:5/10:11: There are several parallels in these two chapters. These verses portray the rejected messengers shaking or wiping the dust of a town off their feet.

The second and third of these instances are good examples of oral formulas. Most, or perhaps all, cultures develop set ways of

---

[17]Cadbury, "Four Features of Lukan Style," 89.

[18]Ibid., 92.

[19]For an overview see the essays collected in John Miles Foley, ed., *Oral-Formulaic Theory: A Folklore Casebook* (New York: Garland Publishing, 1990).

talking about pregnancy and birth that can be characterized as oral formulas. The human response of amazement is recorded regularly as a response to the miracles and sometimes to the teachings of Jesus. The first is a connection between two sets of traditions. The fourth, the shaking of dust, appears to have been a Jewish linguistic formula, describing a ritual cleansing of oneself when leaving a Gentile city.[20]

Cadbury also points out Luke's tendency to use such idiomatic expressions repeatedly in close proximity and then rarely elsewhere. For instance, in 24:31/32/45 the term *dianoigo* (to open or explain) is used in reference to people coming to understand something only after the resurrection of Jesus; the same term shows up in Acts 16:14/17:3. Some such instances can be explained by subject matter, but others leave open the possibility that they are clues to differing oral sources.

Introductory Formulas

In order to record such stories in writing, an author would need to develop ways of getting from the framework narrative to the narrative on the lips of the hero. It is interesting to note that Luke uses idiolectic introductory formulas for the parables. Six times he uses a close variant of *Eipen de parabolen* (6:39; 8:4; 12:16; 15:3; 18:9; 19:11) and three times, *Elegen en de parabolen* (5:36; 13:6; 18:1). Both of these are peculiar Lukan uses.[21] This is the sort of formula that characteristically appears in orally composed material.

Summary and Conclusions

One consistent indicator of the oral source(s) of Luke's gospel is the constant designation of Jesus as a teacher. He is called *didaskale* (teacher) by friend and foe alike in 12:13; 18:18; 19:39; 20:21; 20:27; and 21:7. In 22:11 Jesus calls himself *ho didaskalos* (the teacher). In addition to these titles, the verb form of the same word is used to describe what he is doing in 13:10; 13:22; 19:47; 20:1 (where it is linked with *euangelisomenou*: preaching good news);

---

[20]I. H. Marshall, *The Gospel of Luke: A Commentary on the Greek Text*, New International Greek Testament Commentary (Grand Rapids, Mich.: Eerdmans, 1978), 354.

[21]John C. Hawkins, *Horae Synopticae: Contributions to the Study of the Synoptic Problem* (Grand Rapids, Mich.: Baker Books, 1968), 39.

and 21:37. A teacher in a primarily oral culture does not assign outside readings, nor would one expect disciples to take notes; rather, teaching is done so that the hearers can remember. The primary means for such an appeal to memory are narrative, metaphor, poetically phrased aphorisms, and repetition.[22]

We must understand that the identifying of themes and formulas that we have done here is more difficult in Luke's gospel than in Mark's or Matthew's. Luke has long been recognized as the most literary of the synoptic gospels, and so we need not be surprised to find the marks of orality well hidden and to some extent expunged. Recognizing this, we can be even more deeply impressed with the marks of orality that have become obvious. As indicated earlier, since Luke's gospel appears to be a record of an oral enactment, there can be little doubt that the gospels preserve for posterity and for distant communication the (oral) preaching and teaching of Jesus and the early church.

I see no need to follow Kelber's lead[23] in concluding that the writing down of the previously oral gospel radically changed the nature and impact of that message. It certainly made available another (and different) way of learning and studying that message. However, it did not supplant oral communication, which continues even twenty centuries later. Rather, writing became for the early church one more medium of communication to be used to tell the story of Jesus as effectively and as extensively as possible.

A more important consideration is the nature of the message itself. What sort of word can be communicated in so many different formats without mutilating its meaning? A look at the three primary word roots used to describe the communication process in the early church might help us to better understand this issue. The words *teach, teacher,* and *teaching/doctrine* are so general as to be of little help to us. But the other terms—*proclaim, herald,* and *proclamation,* on the one hand, and *preach good news, evangelist,* and *evangelism* on the other, all point to a sort of promise. To proclaim the kingdom of God where it is invisible or to preach good news

---

[22]See Rainer Riesner, "Jesus as Preacher and Teacher," in *Jesus and the Oral Gospel Tradition,* ed. Henry Wansbrough (Sheffield, England: Sheffield Academic Press, 1991), 185–210.

[23]Kelber, *The Oral and the Written Gospel,* 208: "Mark writes primarily not for the sake of continuing the sayings genre, and not at all to duplicate oral christology, but rather to overcome what are perceived to be problems caused by oral speech and its authoritative carriers."

to people living in pain and poverty is to assure people of a reality either on a different plane of existence or yet in the future. In either case, such a speech act is promise. This will become even more obvious as we investigate the Acts of the Apostles.

4

Preaching and Teaching
in the Acts of the Apostles

Introduction

For some time modern scholars, both critical and fundamentalistic, have appeared unsure about how to approach the Acts of the Apostles. A prevailing devaluing of the church linked with the assumption that Jesus and his earliest followers expected his early return made it difficult for many to imagine a purpose in the first century for writing a history of early Christianity. Some have followed the lead of the Tübingen School of the early nineteenth century to insist that Acts was written later for apologetic purposes. But the way in which the author of Acts chose information and ordered it into a book indicates that he was preparing not just a chronicle of the church from 33 to 60 c.e., but a handbook for posterity, covering methods of preaching, church planting, and congregational ministering. He shows the gospel being proclaimed by different preachers to various audiences in far-flung parts of the empire for several distinct purposes. He describes the effects of these speeches on their hearers. He charts the growth of the church as it spread from Jerusalem to Rome and as it crossed barriers of race, social class, gender, and geography. He develops in the reader an understanding of the way Christians related to one another in the church and how they comported themselves in the larger community. And along the way he guides the reader to grasp the central issues of doctrine and proclamation in early Christianity.

So in the Acts of the Apostles we have not just a historically trustworthy reference work,[1] but more importantly for our purposes, a compendium of the personnel, the content, the format, and the impact of the communication of the gospel in and by the early church.

In the last chapter we looked at an essay by Cadbury in which he deals with both Luke and Acts. We shall follow his lead in our consideration of traces of orality in Acts. In addition, we would be remiss if we overlooked the speeches recorded there. Clearly, those speeches play one of the primary roles in the book of Acts. Scholars have often noted that these addresses in the mouths of several different people betray the style of the author of the book. I contend that the stylistic differences and distinctive doctrinal emphases among them have been too often overlooked, a problem that we might well keep in mind as we proceed.

Repetitions in the Two Volumes

Cadbury lists several instances of repetition between Luke and Acts. An investigation of these repetitions should be helpful.

Luke 1:13/Acts 10:31: "Your prayer has been heard." This assurance is given both to Zechariah in reference to the birth of John and to Cornelius in reference to his hearing the gospel, in each case by an angel.

Luke 1:70/Acts 3:21: "Through [the mouth of] his holy prophets." The first of these coming from the mouth of Zechariah and the second from Peter, both in the Jerusalem temple, indicates a familiar formula for referring to the Old Testament prophets in first-century Judaism. The insertion of "the mouth of" could be a familiar technique of a speaker who needs to add a phrase to stay in the rhythm of the speech.

Luke 2:37/Acts 26:7: "Worshipping night and day." Luke's gospel uses this phrase to describe the prophet Anna, and Acts has Paul using it to describe in a formulaic manner the history of God's people.

---

[1]As has been demonstrated by Martin Hengel, *Acts and the History of Earliest Christianity*, trans. John Bowden (Philadelphia: Fortress Press, 1979).

Luke 17:13/Acts 4:24: *"eran phonen* [they raised voice]." This formulaic way of describing people as raising their voices is clearly repeated in the Greek, though not so noticeably in our translations.

Luke 23:5/Acts 10:37: "Throughout all Judea, from Galilee where he began." This description is repeated almost letter for letter in these two verses, which indicates a strong habitual compunction on the part of the (presumably) oral teller of the tale to use this formula.

These examples of repetition between Luke and Acts are strong evidence, of course, for the common authorship of the two volumes, but such repetitions are also characteristic of oral composition. This is especially remarkable with the work of Luke, who appears to seek to avoid much repetition by changing Mark's wording at times with omissions and synonyms.[2] This indicates what has long been recognized: Luke's work is much more in tune with the developments that accompanied the increase of literacy than is Mark's. Yet even in this double work of Luke, we have strong evidence of an oral source for these carefully literate books.

Story Forms

As we saw in the last chapter, certain story forms (as listed by Kelber) in Luke's gospel appear to function as what scholars of orality call themes. Some of these themes reappear in Acts.

Heroic Stories

Miracle stories compose about 19 percent of the verses in Acts. The persons effecting the miracles here are careful to draw attention to Jesus as the real miracle worker, and the miracles produce opportunities for proclamation, which is generally reported extensively, as can be seen in the following examples.

HEALINGS

3:1—4:4: The first ten of these verses describe the healing of the man, lame from birth, through the ministry of Peter and John at the temple gate. The remaining verses record the sermon of Peter to the crowd that gathers as a result of the miracle.

9:32—35: Here Peter heals the bedridden Aeneas in Lydda in the name of Jesus Christ. Again the condition of the man is described, the healing words "Jesus Christ heals you" are recorded, and the resulting mass conversion is noted.

---

[2]As Cadbury points out on p. 93 of his essay.

9:36–43: In Joppa Peter raises the charitable Dorcas from death. The recognized form appears here also. Some details of Dorcas' life and death appear. Peter is summoned from Joppa, where he has just healed Aeneas. As did Jesus in the raising of the daughter of Jairus (Luke 8), Peter clears the room. He then simply commands Tabitha/Dorcas to get up, which she does. Then "many believed in the Lord."

14:8–18: In Lystra Paul heals a man crippled from birth, which precipitates his and Barnabas' proclaiming the gospel to the people gathered as a result of the miracle.

20:9–12: Because of the way in which this story is told, people have questioned whether we are meant to understand that the young man died, given the normal form of a healing or raising miracle. It appears, however, that first-century hearers would have understood that Paul in Troas raised the young man Eutychus from death after he had fallen from the third-story window. The sequence is broken somewhat here, since there is no report of the responses of the people.

28:7–10: On Malta Paul heals the father of Publius, the leading man of the island. Details are sparse in this report, although the miracle opens opportunities for more powerful acts and, presumably, for the preaching of the gospel.

Miraculous releases

12:1–19: Peter is released from prison in Jerusalem through the miraculous intervention of an angel. The believers are so surprised that they cannot comprehend that it is he. Herod executes the guards.

16:16–34: Paul and Silas are released from prison in Philippi by a miraculous earthquake, but they stay and convert the jailer and his family. So once again a miracle results in conversions.

Polarization Stories

5:1–11: Ananias and his wife, Sapphira, are discovered by Peter to be lying about the proportion of their giving and are struck dead because they are lying to the Holy Spirit. The church is struck with fear.

8:9–24: Philip converts Simon, a magician in Samaria, who later offers Peter and John money for the ability to pass on the miraculous power of the Holy Spirit. Peter curses him, but he repents and asks them to pray for him. Peter and John have great success preaching in Samaria.

9:1–22; 22:3–21; and 26:2–23 (Saul's conversion): Although they differ in some details as is appropriate to differing audiences (and as one would expect of oral repetition), these parallel accounts describe Saul of Tarsus as an early enemy of Christianity who has a miraculous confrontation with the risen Lord on the road to Damascus and who is commissioned by the Lord to proclaim the gospel to the Gentiles, a commission that he spends the rest of his life carrying out.

13:6–12: Paul curses Elymas Bar-Jesus, a magician who is trying to hinder the proclamation of the gospel, and brings on him a temporary blindness, which converts the proconsul of Cyprus.

16:16–18: Paul casts a spirit of divination out of a girl in Philippi; this act becomes the basis for the charge for which he and Silas are imprisoned there.

One of the fascinating aspects of the miracles recorded in Acts is the way in which Luke carefully balances the number of miracles performed through Peter with those done through Paul. As has been shown,[3] this paralleling of the works of Peter and Paul extends even to the summaries in 2:43/14:3 and 5:15/19:12. In the former pair, one finds awe in "everyone" because of the works of Peter and the apostles and then Paul and Barnabas gaining a hearing in Iconium because of the Lord's signs and wonders performed through them. In the latter pair, we find people being healed by being in Peter's shadow and by touching cloths that Paul had touched.

One will also be impressed with how closely Luke links the miracles with the preaching. In nearly every case the miracle occasions preaching, and in a few cases preaching is both at the beginning and at the end of the miracle. In that sense, the miracles in Acts are didactic stories, of which we have several other examples.

Didactic Stories

In Acts, instead of culminating in an epigrammatic statement, these stories usually end with an extensive proclamation of the gospel.

5:27–42: There is a terse, memorable saying here by Gamaliel, who, as a member of the Sanhedrin, is expected to be an enemy of

---

[3]See John A. Hardon, "The Miracle Narratives in the Acts of the Apostles," *Catholic Biblical Quarterly* 16, no. 3 (July 1954): 308f.

the church, but whose wisdom in this case averts further persecution for a time.

6:8—7:60: The case of Stephen begins as a polarization story describing the confrontation between Stephen and a number of Hellenistic Jews, which results in Stephen's being taken before the council. All of this occasions the extended speech by Stephen in which he accuses his accusers and their ancestors of persecuting and killing the prophets and of transgressing the law.

21:26–29: The last two of these didactic stories form a continuous narrative. In this one Paul is accused of desecrating the temple by bringing Greeks into it, an accusation that is explained by both a speech by his accusers and a statement by the narrator.

21:30—22:10: This second part of the story details the spread of the alarm, Paul's being saved from a beating by the intervention of Roman soldiers, and his conversation with the centurion, who then permits him to address the crowd.

Such stories leading to teachings, some of which are reported in detail while others are summarized, are forms familiar to students of orality, who assume that didactic patterns and speeches will be introduced by narratives that describe the situation in which the speech is given.

Repetitions in Acts

Cadbury also points out that there are several extensive repetitions within Acts:

- 10:1–48 is fully summarized in 11:5–17, in Peter's report to the Jerusalem elders. An author careful to avoid redundancy would be expected to describe Peter's defense to the Jerusalem elders by writing (in v. 4) that Peter told them what had happened to him in Joppa and Caesarea. This would suffice for a modern reader, since the whole story was narrated in chapter 10. But very much in the style of oral storytelling, Peter is quoted in full as he describes (*kathekses*: step-by-step) what had happened.

- 9:1–19 (Saul's conversion) is repeated (from the mouth of Paul) in 22:3–16 and 26:4–18. The shock to modern literate sensitivities lies in how widely these repetitions differ in detail. However, this variety is far from shocking to the student of orality, who would expect each performance of a narrative to differ from the others, the distinctives being determined either by different tellers (only two of these three are the mouth of Paul) or by the demands of different audiences.

Therefore, we can see in these repetitions evidence for oral composition. A cursory reading of the epics of Homer or such works as *Beowulf* or *El Cid* should indicate how characteristic of such orally produced texts is this sort of repetition of narrative.

Speeches

Speeches make up about 36 percent of the material in Acts. It appears to have been a common practice at the time to write history by composing/recording speeches by the principal movers of the period. However, Luke's preponderance of speech material points also to the importance of proclamation in the early church.

The following are the speech situations that are presented in Acts as recording the words of the speaker himself.

1:16–22: Peter's brief speech to the gathered disciples is a piece of deliberative rhetoric interrupted by Luke's description (vv. 18–19) of the death of Judas. By his use of biblical authority and reason, Peter convinces the group to select a replacement for Judas among the Twelve.

2:14–40: Peter's Pentecost sermon needs little exegesis for our purposes. In rhetorical terms Peter is shown first defending the disciples against the accusation of drunkenness, then accusing the Jews of crucifying the Messiah. He begins with some typical *pesher midrash*, as used in the Dead Sea Scrolls to apply Old Testament prophecies to specific contemporary situations. He continues with a brief narrative on Jesus' life, crucifixion, and resurrection, which, in good rabbinical fashion, he ties to Psalm 15:8–11, Psalm 16:10, and Psalm 110:1. These pieces of judicial speech are then changed into deliberative rhetoric when Peter responds to the appeal of the crowd with the demand that they repent and be baptized. At this point, the warnings of scripture that he had used earlier are transformed into promises for those who will believe and obey.

3:11–26: Peter's sermon occasioned by the healing of the lame man follows the same rhetorical pattern as the Pentecost sermon. Judicially he shows that it is God's power that has healed the man and that the Jews had killed the Messiah; then he deliberatively transposes the theme of guilt into a promise of grace for those who repent.

4:8–12: Peter and John are before the Sanhedrin, which means that the audience in this situation is much more hostile than in the previous settings. Yet Peter's speech here seems to be basically an abbreviated version of the two previous ones, referring to Psalm 118:22 to accuse the Jews of crucifying their Messiah, and proclaiming salvation only in his name.

5:29–32: Here Luke offers us what appears to be an outline of a speech not unlike the last two, once again before the council. The apostles are here accused of disobeying the injunction of the high priest. Peter, in a forensic argument, transfers the blame to God, who must be obeyed above all earthly powers. This is the familiar Hellenistic rhetorical argument called metastasis, which contends that the present court or judge has no authority in this case.[4] Peter's speech is followed by a brief statement by Gamaliel that, through the use of a hypothetical enthymeme, convinces the council not to take harsh action against the Christians.

7:2–53: This longest of the speeches recorded in Acts is by Stephen, the first Christian martyr, whose death undoubtedly caused a radical change in the activities of the early church and stands in the book of Acts as the transition into the ministry of the apostle Paul, a ministry that extended the gospel to the rest of the Roman Empire. There is, therefore, no reason to doubt that the gist of the speech would have been remembered and passed on by those who heard it. Stephen is accused of seditious statements in his preaching of the gospel of Christ. His defense is basically a denial of the right of the council, who had condemned Jesus to death, to judge him. This is metastasis again. The speech is a rehearsal of the history of Israel ordered in such a way as to prepare the ground for Stephen's accusation of the council. The rhetoric is concluded by Stephen's vision of the Lord, who is the rightful judge, and his Jesus-like prayer (see Lk. 23:34) for forgiveness of his enemies.

10:34–43: As Kennedy points out,[5] this brief report of Peter's speech to the household of Cornelius is the first purely kerygmatic speech in Acts, since it is the first that is free from accusations of the Jews. Here we have the simple telling of the story of Jesus, with only a hint of argumentation in verse 38 ("for God was with him") and a reference to eyewitnesses in verse 39.

---

[4]George A. Kennedy, *New Testament Interpretation through Rhetorical Criticism* (Chapel Hill: University of North Carolina Press, 1984), 120.
[5]Ibid., 122.

13:16–41: Here we have the first missionary speech from the mouth of Paul. It is set in a synagogue in Antioch of Pisidia and is quite credible as an address in such a situation, since it rehearses the history of God's dealing with Israel, presenting it in a way quite acceptable to a Jewish audience. Following this summary of history, Paul presents Jesus as the promised message of salvation by means of his death and resurrection. This he warrants by quoting from Psalm 2, Isaiah 55, and Psalm 16. He then proclaims that through "this man" God is offering forgiveness of sins. Habakkuk 1:5 concludes the sermon as an exhortation not to reject the prophetic word.

14:15–17: This is either a summary of a longer speech or a report of a brief speech. Its context is the healing of a lame man in Lystra, an event that so impressed the pagan witnesses that they prepared to worship Barnabas and his fellow evangelist, Paul. Paul dissuades this action by his speech in which he gives credit to the divine Creator for the miracle. A fuller argument to the mind of the Gentiles awaits in chapter 17.

17:22–31: The sermon by Paul to the philosophers on the Areopagus in Athens appears to be offered by Luke as the primary model of proclamation of the gospel to such an audience. The rhetorical devices expected by one who is familiar with Hellenistic rhetoric are there: the building of rapport with the audience, the references to familiar objects and to traditional statements, and the ordering of material to build an impression in the minds of the hearers. In addition, that ordering seems to be particularly appropriate to the audience, since the claims that would be most difficult to reconcile with their philosophical worldview (especially dualism of matter and spirit and the cyclic view of history) appear at the end of the speech, where it is reported that some scoffed, as would be expected of an audience whose worldview had just been brought into question.[6]

20:18–35: This is the only speech we have reported from the mouth of Paul given to a Christian audience—the elders of the church in Ephesus. The farewell address was a well-known convention in oral narratives as well as in literature, including the Old Testament (see Deuteronomy 32—33 and Josh. 24:19–28). This one is embedded in a passage in which the pronoun *we* points

---

[6]For more on this speech see my "The Areopagus Sermon as a Model for Apologetic Preaching" in *Faith in Practice: Studies in the Book of Acts,* ed. David A. Fiensy and William D. Howden (Tübingen: European Evangelistic Society, 1996), 224–36.

to an eyewitness account. The personal nature of the address, its impeccable rhetorical structure, and its similarity to the style of Paul's epistles are evidence that we are close here to the actual words of the apostle.

22:1–21: This judicial speech by Paul to defend himself before the Jewish crowd in the temple is introduced with the expected gestures and words of the orator. The content repeats largely the account in chapter 9 of Paul's experience on the road to Damascus. As noted above, the few minor discrepancies reflect the flexibility permitted to the teller of tales in a primarily oral culture.

24:10–21: In yet another defense Paul uses the format and the techniques of argumentation common to such speeches. He presents no evidence, but points out that his accusers have none either. He admits to being a Christian and to speaking about the resurrection of the dead, but there was no law against either one. He makes it clear that the whole dispute centers on Jewish religious concerns over which the Romans have no jurisdiction (another use of metastasis). He clearly denies having desecrated the temple, which was the main contention of his accusers.

26:1–29: Here we have Paul's defense before King Agrippa, who was much better prepared than Festus or Felix, the Roman governors, to appreciate Paul's situation and to understand his story. Again we note the expected format and niceties of Hellenistic rhetoric, this time supported by references that might have appealed to Agrippa: the Lord's having spoken to Paul in Hebrew (v. 14) and reference to the prophets and Moses (v. 22). The neatness of the rhetoric is interrupted by Festus (v. 24), which is an interesting narrator's device.

28:25–28: These words of Paul appear to be the conclusion to an extended argument between him and the Jewish leaders in Rome. Here he quotes Isaiah 6:9–10 and announces that the gospel will be heard by the Gentiles.

We should also note the consistent content of the various speeches recorded in Acts. In the sermons by Peter, Philip, Stephen, and Paul the central theme is the death and resurrection of Jesus. The one possible exception is Paul's sermon on the Areopagus (17:22–31), but even here Luke notes that the proclamation of the resurrection of the dead (which obviously presupposes death) is what causes the philosophers to scoff. In addition to this central theme, which is repeated tirelessly, we see a consistent extending of this good news of what God has done as a promise from God— the promise of forgiveness or salvation linked with the necessity of a total change of mind (repentance). Peter's Pentecost sermon is very explicit:

> Repent, and be baptized every one of you in the name of Jesus Christ so that your sins may be forgiven; and you will receive the gift of the Holy Spirit. For the promise is for you, for your children, and for all who are far away, everyone whom the Lord our God calls to him. (2:38–39)

We shall return in chapter 7 to the implications of the preaching of the gospel as promise. In the meantime, we should keep in mind that not only the Pentecost sermon, but also, perhaps less explicitly, the other mission sermons in Acts do more than report on an event; they proclaim the event as an offer from God to every human being.

There are a number of other speeches mentioned in Acts, some of which are reported in summary fashion (chapter 15) and some of which are by less-than-primary figures in the story (Herod, Tertullus). Those surveyed above, however, are rather fully reported and play decisive roles in the story.

Summary and Conclusion

Without disagreeing with the prevailing view that the author of Acts has unified the style of the work by reporting the results of his research in his own literary style, we can still recognize the marks of oral traditions behind the finished product. The formulaic and thematic communication that we have surveyed, added to the preponderance of recorded speeches, offer us glimpses of a writer who listened carefully to the oral reports of his contemporaries so as to record their anecdotes accurately, along with his personal recollections of both events and speeches.

It is obvious that Luke had a definite purpose in mind as he set down these traditions of earliest Christianity. His decision to close the book with a non-ending statement ("proclaiming...and teaching...without hindrance" [Acts 28:31]) indicates that he intends the story to continue unfolding in the experience of the church. Thus, his book functions as a reference work, so that later Christians can know how the work of evangelism and church planting were done during the apostolic age.

It is equally obvious that those later Christians (us included) are expected to find here a clear picture of the process in that age of Christian origins of passing on the tradition of Christ. Luke has described and, to some extent, defined that tradition in his

gospel, and in Acts he has shown how various tellers communicated it to various hearers and how they were all affected by
the process. In a later chapter we shall return to an analysis of the
nature of this communication process in order to determine
whether it can be useful to us today. In the meantime we will
complete our survey of the New Testament material and look at
contemporary preaching.

5

Pointers to Oral Communication in the Epistles

Given what we now know about the primary orality of the first-century culture, we can understand something about the communication patterns of the earliest Christians. We should recognize that even a literate person like the apostle Paul would still assume that human language was essentially sounds and that writing was merely a "modern" technique by which to preserve and transport acts of language.

Given this cultural context, we can assume that for Paul writing would not seem unusual but that even the writing was expected to be heard (not read silently). And given his primary occupation as preacher/teacher, we should expect that Paul's references to evangelization, the gospel, the word (either *logos* or *rhema*), the kerygma, and other linguistic terms would presuppose oral presentation and aural reception. This lifts many of Paul's statements out of the realm of the abstract and fits them back into his own daily activities.

An exhaustive survey of the Pauline materials is unnecessary here, so we will look briefly at statements in Romans, 1 and 2 Corinthians, Galatians, and 1 Thessalonians. Our concern is not a complete exegesis of the relevant passages, but an understanding of what Paul says in them about oral communication. Following this survey of Paul's writings, we shall look at statements in other epistles that point to orally transmitted information.[1]

References to Paul's Own Ministry

In several passages the apostle discusses aspects of his own ministry that involve communication. After looking at these texts, we will look at some more general references to proclamation, to the law, and to the church.

Romans 1:1–5 (cf. 15:18–20 and 16:25–27), 1:9, 15, 16–17:

Paul, a servant of Jesus Christ, called to be an apostle, set apart for the gospel of God, which he promised beforehand through his prophets in the holy scriptures, the gospel concerning his Son, who was descended from David according to the flesh and was declared to be Son of God with power according to the spirit of holiness by resurrection from the dead, Jesus Christ our Lord, through whom we have received grace and apostleship to bring about the obedience of faith among all the Gentiles for the sake of his name…For God, whom I serve with my spirit by announcing the gospel of his Son, is my witness that without ceasing I remember you always in my prayers,…hence my eagerness to proclaim the gospel to you also who are in Rome.

   For I am not ashamed of the gospel; it is the power of God for salvation to everyone who has faith, to the Jew first and also to the Greek. For in it the righteousness of God is revealed through faith for faith; as it is written, "The one who is righteous will live by faith."

In light of our developing understanding of primarily oral cultures there should be no doubt that Paul could hardly have used terms like *euangelion* (good news) or *kerugma* (proclamation) with reference only to what we call the content of the communication. It seems self-defeating to argue that it is the content or message of the gospel or of the proclamation that is uppermost in his mind. There is, of course, no indication that he saw preaching as a magical act by which persons are saved, as

---

[1]For an excellent and much more complete treatment of orality in Paul's letters see John D. Harvey, *Listening to the Text: Oral Patterning in Paul's Letters* (Grand Rapids, Mich.: Baker Books, 1998). This book came to my attention too late to incorporate much of Harvey's research into my more modest work.

was developed in some later attempts to contextualize the gospel (God's spell)[2]; it is the grace of God in Christ that justifies human beings. But the transmission of that saving fact is a necessary aspect of the fact itself. So when Paul, in Romans, refers to the gospel (Rom. 1:1, 9, and 16, as well as 15:19 and 16:25) or to preaching the gospel (1:15; 15:19) or to the proclamation (16:26), he is referring to the act of preaching the good news about or announcing the fact of the gracious act of God in Christ for the salvation of human beings.

It is in this context that Paul chooses to identify this gospel as God's power for the salvation of all people. As we shall see below, Paul had in common with the saints in Corinth some experiences that permitted him to be more specific about the power of God in this preaching. Here in Romans he chose to write generally about the preached gospel as the vehicle for the revelation of God's justification, which, as I understand Paul,[3] originates in God's faithfulness (*ek pisteos*) and which aims to be received by the sinner's faith (*eis pistin*). To this "gospel of God" the apostle understands himself, according to Romans 1:1, to be set apart. The oral communication of the good news of God is Paul's divinely ordained purpose in life.

First Corinthians 1:17–25; 2:1–7

For Christ did not send me to baptize but to proclaim the gospel, and not with eloquent wisdom, so that the cross of Christ might not be emptied of its power.

For the message about the cross is foolishness to those who are perishing, but to us who are being saved it is the power of God. For it is written,

"I will destroy the wisdom of the wise, and the discernment of the discerning I will thwart."

Where is the one who is wise? Where is the scribe? Where is the debater of this age? Has not God made foolish the wisdom of the world? For since, in the wisdom of God, the world did not know God through wisdom, God decided, through the foolishness of our proclamation, to save those who believe. For Jews demand signs and Greeks desire wisdom, but we proclaim Christ crucified, a

---

[2]This is true in *The Heliand*, the Saxon gospel dating back to the ninth century. See the new translation of it by G. Ronald Murphy (New York and Oxford: Oxford University Press, 1992).

[3]Bruce E. Shields, *Romans* (Cincinnati: Standard, 1988), 25.

stumbling block to Jews and foolishness to Gentiles, but to those who are the called, both Jews and Greeks, Christ the power of God and the wisdom of God. For God's foolishness is wiser than human wisdom, and God's weakness is stronger than human strength...

When I came to you, brothers and sisters, I did not come proclaiming the mystery of God to you in lofty words or wisdom. For I decided to know nothing among you except Jesus Christ, and him crucified. And I came to you in weakness and in fear and in much trembling. My speech and my proclamation were not with plausible words of wisdom, but with a demonstration of the Spirit and of power, so that your faith might rest not on human wisdom but on the power of God.

Yet among the mature we do speak wisdom, though it is not a wisdom of this age or of the rulers of this age, who are doomed to perish. But we speak God's wisdom, secret and hidden, which God decreed before the ages for our glory.

Here Paul continues to refer to his ministry, first by challenging the wise person, the literate person, and the skillful debater (*pou sophos; pou grammateus; pou suzetetes*, 1:20) with the wisdom of God, who has chosen the foolishness of preaching (*dia tes morias tou kerugmatos*) as the agency of salvation. His own preaching, he points out in verse 17, was not wisdom as oratory (*en sophia logou*), which the Corinthians would have recognized as the method of many contemporary philosophers.[4] He contrasts that deceptive wisdom with the cross as the power of God (v. 18) and the wisdom of God (v. 21). Verses 23 and 24 clearly define the content of the preaching as the real means of salvation, but it seems clear that Paul understands that the story must be articulated and heard if it is to be effective. Then Paul proceeds in 2:1–7 to make clear that it is not in any subtle trickery of oratory that the gospel does its work, but in the simple (*ho logos mou*: my word) announcement (*to kerugma mou*: my proclamation) of "Jesus Christ, and him crucified." This announcement, he reminds them, was accompanied by a demonstration of power that could have been

---

[4]John William Beaudean, Jr., *Paul's Theology of Preaching* (Macon, Ga.: Mercer University Press, 1988), 93f. See also Andre Resner, Jr., *Preacher and Cross: Person and Message in Theology and Rhetoric* (Grand Rapids, Mich.: Eerdmans, 1999), 9–37 and 83–132.

accomplished only by God. The seemingly foolish weakness of announcing the salvation of the world through a crucified Galilean while rejecting the common tricks of oratory in which to dress the announcement could be convincing only if accompanied by the power of God.[5] Since both the message and the medium appeared either ordinary or downright foolish, the manifest effectiveness of the gospel in radically changing the lives of those who received it in faith could be credited only to the power of God. This appears to be the purpose of Paul's emphasizing the unremarkable and sometimes repulsive lives these people had led before coming to faith in Christ.

Second Corinthians 4:1–6

> Therefore, since it is by God's mercy that we are engaged in this ministry, we do not lose heart. We have renounced the shameful things that one hides; we refuse to practice cunning or to falsify God's word; but by the open statement of the truth we commend ourselves to the conscience of everyone in the sight of God. And even if our gospel is veiled, it is veiled to those who are perishing. In their case the god of this world has blinded the minds of the unbelievers, to keep them from seeing the light of the gospel of the glory of Christ, who is the image of God. For we do not proclaim ourselves; we proclaim Jesus Christ as Lord and ourselves as your slaves for Jesus' sake. For it is the God who said, "Let light shine out of darkness," who has shone in our hearts to give the light of the knowledge of the glory of God in the face of Jesus Christ.

In 2 Corinthians Paul turns to cases about his ministry, which appears to have been belittled or directly attacked by his opponents in Corinth. What he says in chapter 4 is relevant to our discussion. Here he denies any trickery or deception in his treatment of the word of God; he describes his method rather as simply and openly stating the truth (*te phanerosei tes aletheias*, v. 2b). He goes on to say that whatever lack of clarity (veiling) of the gospel happens is the work of "the god of this world," who attempts to keep people "from seeing the light of the gospel of the glory of Christ, who is the image of God" (v. 4).

---

[5]Beaudean, *Paul's Theology*, 104.

Paul next employs the term *kerusso* again to point out that the message that he proclaims is not himself but rather "Jesus Christ as Lord and ourselves as your slaves for Jesus' sake" (v. 5). We will see more of this connection of the person and character of the preacher with the content of the message when we turn to Galatians. Paul brings this 2 Corinthians passage to a close by jumping from the proclamation of Christ to God's creating light out of darkness by speaking (*ho eipon*: the one who said). What appears to the normal human being as weakness, that is, trusting a simple announcement of facts and claims about a crucified man to lead the human race to salvation, Paul puts in the framework of the creative power of the God who brought the whole universe into being with his voice. Thus, the human voice that is employed in the proclamation of this gospel is borne on the breath of God himself.

Galatians 1:6–12; 3:1–6

I am astonished that you are so quickly deserting the one who called you in the grace of Christ and are turning to a different gospel—not that there is another gospel, but there are some who are confusing you and want to pervert the gospel of Christ. But even if we or an angel from heaven should proclaim to you a gospel contrary to what we proclaimed to you, let that one be accursed! As we have said before, so now I repeat, if anyone proclaims to you a gospel contrary to what you received, let that one be accursed!

Am I now seeking human approval, or God's approval? Or am I trying to please people? If I were still pleasing people, I would not be a servant of Christ.

For I want you to know, brothers and sisters, that the gospel that was proclaimed by me is not of human origin; for I did not receive it from a human source, nor was I taught it, but I received it through a revelation of Jesus Christ.

…You foolish Galatians! Who has bewitched you? It was before your eyes that Jesus Christ was publicly exhibited as crucified! The only thing I want to learn from you is this: Did you receive the Spirit by doing the works of the law or by believing what you heard? Are you so foolish? Having started with the Spirit, are you now ending with the flesh? Did you experience so much for nothing?—if it really was for nothing. Well then, does God supply you with the Spirit and work miracles among you by your doing the works of the law, or by your believing what you heard?

Just as Abraham "believed God, and it was reckoned to him as righteousness."

The multiple mentions in Galatians 1:6–12 of gospel and preaching the gospel, which are noun and verb forms of the same root, indicate the centrality of the spoken transmission of the story in Paul's ministry. The pains Paul takes in these early verses of Galatians to defend his character and his calling indicate the linking of the character of the gospel with the character of the preacher. In fact, 2:14 indicates that there is a way of living that corresponds to what Paul calls the truth of the gospel—a correspondence important enough to cause Paul to confront Cephas (Peter) with his inconsistency. Such a connection between character and persuasion is not unusual,[6] but the nature of the Christian gospel makes it an integral part of the communication process. It is hardly coincidental that the several writers of New Testament documents all emphasize in one way or another the necessity of verbal honesty on the part of every Christian in every situation of life.[7] Christ is understood as God's word, and the salvation of the human race now depends on belief in the words about him; therefore, credibility is a central concern.

Galatians 3 opens with a graphic description of this communication as the portrayal of Jesus Christ as crucified before their very eyes. This defines not an orator's argument designed to convince hearers (although Aristotle also deals with description),[8] but rather a storyteller's describing a scene so vividly that the hearer seems actually to be there. This paragraph also includes two references (vv. 2 and 5) to faith as arising out of hearing (*ex akoes pisteos*), which is closely related to Romans 10:17, to which we shall return below.

---

[6]See Aristotle, *Rhetoric*, Bk. 3, chap. 19, and Resner, *Preacher and Cross.*

[7]We have already noted the story of Ananias and Sapphira. See also the strong statement in James 3:1–12.

[8]Aristotle, *Rhetoric*, Bk. 3, chap. 11.

First Thessalonians 1:2–10; 2:1–14

We always give thanks to God for all of you and mention you in our prayers, constantly remembering before our God and Father your work of faith and labor of love and steadfastness of hope in our Lord Jesus Christ. For we know, brothers and sisters beloved by God, that he has chosen you, because our message of the gospel came to you not in word only, but also in power and in the Holy Spirit and with full conviction; just as you know what kind of persons we proved to be among you for your sake. And you became imitators of us and of the Lord, for in spite of persecution you received the word with joy inspired by the Holy Spirit, so that you became an example to all the believers in Macedonia and in Achaia. For the word of the Lord has sounded forth from you not only in Macedonia and Achaia, but in every place your faith in God has become known, so that we have no need to speak about it. For the people of those regions report about us what kind of welcome we had among you, and how you turned to God from idols, to serve a living and true God, and to wait for his Son from heaven, whom he raised from the dead—Jesus, who rescues us from the wrath that is coming.

You yourselves know, brothers and sisters, that our coming to you was not in vain, but though we had already suffered and been shamefully mistreated at Philippi, as you know, we had courage in our God to declare to you the gospel of God in spite of great opposition. For our appeal does not spring from deceit or impure motives or trickery, but just as we have been approved by God to be entrusted with the message of the gospel, even so we speak, not to please mortals, but to please God who tests our hearts. As you know and as God is our witness, we never came with words of flattery or with a pretext for greed; nor did we seek praise from mortals, whether from you or from others, though we might have made demands as apostles of Christ. But we were gentle among you, like a nurse tenderly caring for her own children. So deeply do we care for you that we are determined to share with you not only the gospel of God but also our own selves, because you have become very dear to us.

> You remember our labor and toil, brothers and sisters; we worked night and day, so that we might not burden any of you while we proclaimed to you the gospel of God. You are witnesses, and God also, how pure, upright, and blameless our conduct was toward you believers. As you know, we dealt with each one of you like a father with his children, urging and encouraging you and pleading that you lead a life worthy of God, who calls you into his own kingdom and glory.
>
> We also constantly give thanks to God for this, that when you received the word of God that you heard from us, you accepted it not as a human word but as what it really is, God's word, which is also at work in you believers. For you, brothers and sisters, became imitators of the churches of God in Christ Jesus that are in Judea, for you suffered the same things from your own compatriots as they did from the Jews.

In this pericope, Paul extols the believers in Thessalonica first by reminding them of how they received the word that he had preached to them and then by complimenting them on how the word was going forth from them. In verse 5, Paul describes their conversion in terms of the gospel happening among them (*to euangelion hemon sukegenethe eis humas en logo monon*) not in word alone. This event nature of the act of communication is a common theme in the Hebrew Scriptures, especially in the prophets.[9] It also underlies much of the talk about communication in the New Testament, as well as the descriptions of preaching in both the gospels and the book of Acts. For Paul such power in communication is due to the activity of the Holy Spirit and the character of the preacher. This power, Paul indicates in verses 9 and 10, is displayed in the changes obvious in the lives of the receivers: their rejection of idols, service of the living God, and their hope of rescue from the coming wrath.

After Paul opens chapter 2 with a reminder of his character as the one from whom they first heard the gospel, he describes

---

[9]Isaiah 55:10–11: "For as the rain and the snow come down from heaven, and do not return there until they have watered the earth, making it bring forth and sprout, giving seed to the sower and bread to the eater, so shall my word be that goes out of my mouth; it shall not return to me empty, but it shall accomplish that which I purpose, and succeed in the thing for which I sent it."

(v. 13) their reception of that proclamation. What they received he calls *logon akoes par' hemon tou theou* (word of hearing [or report] from us of God). Whatever else he might mean by that statement, it seems clear "that the nature of preaching is essentially *oral*."[10] Paul's main point here is that they recognized in this oral, human communication the very word of God, which went to work in their lives to change and empower them for the persecutions that lay ahead.

Paul insisted that the good news/proclamation was the primary focus of his ministry. Those acts of human speech became, in his experience, God's chosen and powerful means of salvation for those who heard them rightly. We must recognize that any attempt on our part to define *euangelion* or *kerugma* as some abstract idea or body of doctrine independent of oral communication is a departure from Paul's own understanding.

General References to Proclamation

In these passages, Paul deals with the nature of gospel proclamation. A look into these texts should help to clarify our thinking about the communication of the Christian faith by Paul and other early Christians.

Romans 10:5–18

Moses writes concerning the righteousness that comes from the law, that "the person who does these things will live by them." But the righteousness that comes from faith says, "Do not say in your heart, 'Who will ascend into heaven?'" (that is, to bring Christ down) "or 'Who will descend into the abyss?'" (that is, to bring Christ up from the dead). But what does it say?

"The word is near you,
on your lips and in your heart"

(that is, the word of faith that we proclaim); because if you confess with your lips that Jesus is Lord and believe in your heart that God raised him from the dead, you will be saved. For one believes with the heart and so is justified, and one confesses with the mouth and so is saved. The scripture says, "No one who believes in him will be put to shame." For there is no distinction between Jew and Greek;

---

[10]Beaudean, *Paul's Theology*, 54f., his emphasis.

the same Lord is Lord of all and is generous to all who call on him. For, "Everyone who calls on the name of the Lord shall be saved."

But how are they to call on one in whom they have not believed? And how are they to believe in one of whom they have never heard? And how are they to hear without someone to proclaim him? And how are they to proclaim him unless they are sent? As it is written, "How beautiful are the feet of those who bring good news!" But not all have obeyed the good news; for Isaiah says, "Lord, who has believed our message?" So faith comes from what is heard, and what is heard comes through the word of Christ.

But I ask, have they not heard? Indeed they have; for

"Their voice has gone out to all the earth,
and their words to the ends of the world."

In Romans 10, Paul is concerned with the communication and reception of the gospel. In this central section of the chapter, we find Paul putting himself in the place of Moses preparing his people for their entrance into the promised land. The apostle paraphrases and explains for his people the words of the lawgiver—words that Paul uses to refer to the incarnate and risen Word of God and "the word of faith that we proclaim" (v. 8). The combination of believing with the heart and confessing with the mouth is the means of salvation (v. 10). This leaves the human race with the necessity of hearing what they need to believe and confess, which prompts Paul to think about and quote part of Isaiah 53, "Who has believed what we have heard?" This query, which begins the chapter in Isaiah, uses the Hebrew term *shemu'a,* which the Septuagint translates *akoe* (the report or what we heard). This is the translation Paul uses in verse 16 and the word he uses twice again in verse 17, where we find what is his most challenging statement about preaching: *ara he pistis ex akoes, he de akoe dia rhematos Christou* ("So faith comes from what is heard [or hearing], and what is heard comes through the word of Christ."). It appears that in much the same way that the Hebrew word *shema* (see Deut. 6:4) came to play an exceedingly important role in the life of Israel and in the lives of individual Jews, so Paul sees *akoe* playing a decisive role in the process of salvation for Christians. Hearing the report of what God has done in Christ is essential to saving faith. Thus, to be heard, the reporting must be more than just a human activity; Paul explains that the real means of such hearing is the very expression of Christ himself (*dia rhematos Christou*), which in this context is closely related to (identical with?) the word (*rhema*, v. 8), which Moses said was "on your lips and in your heart."

In this Romans 10 discussion, Paul brings together his communication vocabulary in a way that indicates his attitude toward preaching. The word of God dominates the chapter, starting with Moses (the use of *rhema* in the Septuagint translation of Deut. 30:14 apparently determines his vocabulary here) and including quotations from both Isaiah and Psalms. That word is pictured as being proclaimed (*to rhema tes pisteos ho kerussomen*: the word of faith we proclaim, v. 8b, cf. v. 14), which draws attention to the communicator as one who is given a message and sent to deliver it. Even though we hear (and read) much more about the term *logos*, it appears that the church continued to use *rhema* to draw attention to the immediate, personal spoken word. Douglas Burton-Christie indicates that it is a common term also in *Sayings of the Desert Fathers*, that compendium of words from fourth-century Egyptian monks, whose disciples would request a word from a master by saying, "*Eipe moi rhema*." He continues:

> The word *rhema* corresponds to the Hebrew *dabar* and has a similar connotation of a deed or an "event" which is announced by a word. It expresses both the close relation between life and action which characterized these words as well as the weight and authority they possessed. Furthermore, it was commonly understood in the desert that one did not speak these words apart from an inspiration from God, nor did one convey such a word to a listener unless that person showed a willingness to put the word into action.[11]

As we have seen, in Romans 10, Paul shows the correspondence between *rhema* and *shema*, which magnifies the weight of the term in early Christianity.

Paul emphasizes the nature of the message by employing the term *euangelion*, first in verb form in the quotation of Isaiah 52:7

---

[11]Burton-Christie, *The Word in the Desert*, 77f.

in verse 15, then in noun form in verse 16. As is commonly known, this word means good news. The participation of the hearers in the communication process is underlined by the use of the terms *pisteuo* (believe) and *akoe* (hearing/report). The quotation of Isaiah 53:1 in verse 16 leaves the impression that the prophetic word is first heard by the prophet and then reported to the people, who then make a judgment about it.[12] A positive judgment is faith or belief, while a negative judgment would be rejection. So then, if one hears aright faith will result (v. 17). That faith will be expressed by a confession that Jesus is Lord (v. 9), which leads to justification and salvation (v. 10).

Here we see that the apostle Paul understands his work of communication of the gospel as more than human oratory; he sees it as guided and empowered by Christ himself, so that the power (Rom. 1:16; 1 Cor. 2:5) is to be credited to God. He also sees it as working with divine power in the process of calling the human race back to God.

First Corinthians 15:1–11

> Now I would remind you, brothers and sisters, of the good news that I proclaimed to you, which you in turn received, in which also you stand, through which also you are being saved, if you hold firmly to the message that I proclaimed to you—unless you have come to believe in vain.
>
> For I handed on to you as of first importance what I in turn had received: that Christ died for our sins in accordance with the scriptures, and that he was buried, and that he was raised on the third day in accordance with the scriptures, and that he appeared to Cephas, then to the twelve. Then he appeared to more than five hundred brothers and sisters at one time, most of whom are still alive, though some have died. Then he appeared to James, then to all the apostles. Last of all, as to one untimely born, he appeared also to me. For I am the least of the apostles, unfit to be called an apostle, because I persecuted the church of God. But by the grace of God I am what I am, and his grace toward me has not been in vain. On the contrary, I worked harder than any of them—though it

---

[12]Cf. J. Christiaan Beker, *Paul the Apostle: The Triumph of God in Life and Thought* (Philadelphia: Fortress Press, 1980), 122.

was not I, but the grace of God that is with me. Whether then it was I or they, so we proclaim and so you have come to believe.

As noted at the beginning of chapter 3, this statement of the gospel by Paul is structured in what we today would consider a logical way. It lists facts of history and people who could verify those facts. By using a term of oral tradition (*parelabete*: you received), as he does also in 1 Corinthians 11:23, he draws attention again to the oral nature of the proclamation. He reminds the Corinthian Christians that he had announced it, that they had received it, and that they stand in salvation through it if they hold firmly to it. He then repeats the message in summary fashion. I see no reason to think that this is the format in which he would have preached, since what he summarizes here is the sequence of the primary acts of a narrative, which would most naturally have been preached as a story, explained where necessary, and connected in whatever way would be appropriate to a life story with which the hearers could identify.

We see, then, that the nature of the report that must be heard is a story of God's acting on behalf of humankind in a powerful way in the life, death, and resurrection of the Christ. Since this matches Paul's briefer depictions of the gospel (Rom. 4:25; Gal. 3:1), we may assume that when he refers to proclamation or evangelization, it is to the telling of this story that he has reference.

Contrast between the Written Law and Faith

It was not unusual in Greek political thought to speak of written and unwritten laws. In fact, during the pre-Christian development of government in both Greek and Roman circles, the unwritten law was often considered more weighty than the written. Sophocles' drama *Antigone* is a good example of this attitude.[13] Antigone becomes a hero figure by defying the written law and honoring the unwritten law by giving her brother a decent burial. However, Paul's contrasting of the written law with faith appears to be somewhat distinctive. Instead of commonly recognized customs and values, he holds up the peculiar

---

[13]See Rosalind Thomas, *Literacy and Orality in Ancient Greece* (Cambridge: Cambridge University Press, 1992), chap. 7.

relationship that Christians have with God through Christ as that which supersedes the written code.

Romans 3:19–31 and 7:1–14 make it clear, in fact, that Paul's contrast has very little to do with written or unwritten law. His point is that every attempt to establish a relationship with God by obedience to law (even law written on the heart, Rom. 2:14–16) is bound to fail, while God is eager to establish such a relationship by his gracious act in the death and resurrection of Jesus, made known by the verbal proclamation of it. Where Paul does mention writing, it is to set up the contrast between the dead letter of the law and the dynamic spirit of God (Rom. 7:6).

A similar but more pointed contrast is made in 2 Corinthians 3:6b–11. Here too the contrast is between the letter and the Spirit. The letter he connects with death (vv. 6–7), fading glory (vv. 7–11), and condemnation (v. 9), while he connects the Spirit with life (v. 6), permanent glory (vv. 8–11), and justification (v. 9).

It is certainly possible that the etymological connection in both Hebrew and Greek between terms for spirit and breath or wind made Paul (consciously or unconsciously) connect spirit with oral communication rather than with written letters, but this sort of thinking is impossible to prove. Whatever the case, Paul is consistent in his conviction that oral proclamation is accompanied by the Holy Spirit and power.

References to the Ministry of the Church

One cannot help being impressed with the number of times terms dealing with oral communication and communicators appear in lists of functions of the church and its leaders in the writings of Paul. The following are only the most obvious.

Romans 12:6–8

We have gifts that differ according to the grace given to us: prophecy, in proportion to faith; ministry, in ministering; the teacher, in teaching; the exhorter, in exhortation; the giver, in generosity; the leader, in diligence; the compassionate, in cheerfulness.

Here the apostle lists seven gifts (*charismata*) that are found and exercised in the church. Three of the seven are explicitly speech activities (prophecy, teaching, and exhorting) and two of the others could include speaking responsibilities (ministering and leading).

First Corinthians 12:8–10 (and chapter 14)

> To one is given through the Spirit the utterance of wisdom,
> and to another the utterance of knowledge according to
> the same Spirit, to another faith by the same Spirit, to
> another gifts of healing by the one Spirit, to another the
> working of miracles, to another prophecy, to another the
> discernment of spirits, to another various kinds of tongues,
> to another the interpretation of tongues.

In 1 Corinthians 12 we have this other list of gifts given for
the common good of the church. Of the nine gifts mentioned, five
(utterance of wisdom, utterance of knowledge, prophecy, various
tongues, and interpretation of tongues) are definitely voice related.
The others (faith, healing, miracles, and discernment of spirits)
could have speech components.

The whole of chapter 14 is devoted to what appears to have
become a major problem in Corinth, the practice of speaking in
tongues and what Paul sees as its revelatory counterpart,
prophesying. Paul upholds the validity of both activities, while
emphasizing the primacy of the word that is understood by people
in general. We need not go into more detail on these issues here.
For our present purpose it is enough to note the extreme
importance of speech both within the church and by the church
to those outside it.

Other Epistle Texts

These same trends toward the recognition of the primary
importance of the spoken word in the church appear in most of
the other epistles of the New Testament. A few examples should
be enough to illustrate how general the tendency is.

The request for prayer that closes Ephesians (6:19–20) asks
that prayer be offered for the author, that (literally) "a word be
given me in the opening of my mouth in boldness [or frankness
of speech] to make known the mystery of the gospel." He then
reiterates the need for bold or frank speech, "that I may say it
boldly as it is necessary for me to speak."[14] In a similar vein but
directed to the work of others is the statement in Philippians 1:14,
where most fellow Christians are shown to be speaking "the word
with greater boldness and without fear" because of Paul's
imprisonment.

---

[14]Author's translation.

Colossians 1:23 emphasizes that the gospel that brought the recipients hope was a message they heard and that was being proclaimed in all creation (or among all creatures). In the third chapter of that epistle (vv. 8 and 9) the Colossians are warned to rid themselves of "anger, wrath, malice, slander, and abusive language from your mouth." They are also exhorted not to lie to one another. As we shall see, terms relating to speech commonly appear also in lists of vices in the New Testament.

According to 1 Timothy 5:17, double honor is to be accorded especially to elders who labor in the word and teaching. Second Timothy puts an even greater emphasis on speech. In 2:14 people are warned not to wrangle over words, since it tends to ruin (*katastrophe*) the ones listening. In 4:2 Paul exhorts Timothy to proclaim the word, and 4:3 explains that people will have "itching ears" and "will turn away from listening to the truth." Titus 1:2–3 emphasizes the process of God's promise being revealed in proclamation, while verse 9 instructs that the Christian leader should be able both to exhort "with sound doctrine and to refute those who contradict it."

The epistle to the Hebrews begins with that wonderful passage describing how "God spoke to our ancestors in many and various ways by the prophets, but in these last days he has spoken to us by a Son," who "sustains all things by his powerful word." In chapter 4 the author returns to the theme of the spoken word in verses 2 and 12. Verse 2 emphasizes the difference between hearing and listening in faith, and verse 12 describes God's word as "living and active, sharper than any two-edged sword, piercing until it divides soul from spirit, joints from marrow; it is able to judge the thoughts and intentions of the heart."

James warns in no uncertain terms in chapter 3 (vv. 1–10) about the dangers of the misuse of the tongue:

> Not many of you should become teachers, my brothers and sisters, for you know that we who teach will be judged with greater strictness. For all of us make many mistakes. Anyone who makes no mistakes in speaking is perfect, able to keep the whole body in check with a bridle. If we put bits into the mouths of horses to make them obey us, we guide their whole bodies. Or look at ships: though they are so large that it takes strong winds to drive them, yet they are guided by a very small rudder wherever the will of the pilot directs. So also the tongue is a small member, yet it boasts of great exploits.

How great a forest is set ablaze by a small fire! And the tongue is a fire. The tongue is placed among our members as a world of iniquity; it stains the whole body, sets on fire the cycle of nature, and is itself set on fire by hell. For every species of beast and bird, of reptile and sea creature, can be tamed and has been tamed by the human species, but no one can tame the tongue—a restless evil, full of deadly poison. With it we bless the Lord and Father, and with it we curse those who are made in the likeness of God. From the same mouth come blessing and cursing. My brothers and sisters, this ought not to be so.

First Peter 1:25 quotes from Isaiah 40 "but the word (*rhema*) of the Lord endures forever," and then points out that this "word is the good news that was announced to you." First Peter 4:11 has the breathtaking exhortation, "Whoever speaks must do so as one speaking the very words (*logia*) of God." Then in the familiar passage 2 Peter 1:21, we find the working of the prophets described as people who "moved by the Holy Spirit spoke from God." First John reiterates some of these same themes, as one sees in the repeated references to hearing and announcing in 1:1–5 and the emphasis on lying as the basic sin of humanity.

Jude 17–18 brings to our attention another factor—the use of orally transmitted statements from Jesus and the apostles. Here Jude refers to the apostles who said, "In the last time there will be scoffers, indulging their own ungodly lusts." This statement does not appear in any other New Testament document, which means that the writer assumes that his recipients have heard this statement passed on to them through the process of the oral retelling of the stories and statements of the apostles. Luke gives us a similar glimpse of the oral tradition of Jesus in Paul's speech to the Ephesian elders in Acts 20:35, where he reports Paul as quoting the Lord Jesus as having said, "It is more blessed to give than to receive." This statement seems very much in place in the teaching of Jesus, but we find it documented only in this speech of Paul.

It will be quite appropriate for us to close this part of our study with words from the opening chapter of Revelation: "Blessed is the one who reads aloud the words of the prophecy, and blessed are those who hear and who keep what is written in it; for the time is near" (v. 3).

Summary

It seems obvious that Paul understands the power of the gospel as residing not just in the "content" of the message, since the distinguishing of content from sound would have seemed a strange process of abstraction in a culture of primary orality. Rather Paul writes about the gospel as becoming effective through God's empowerment in the act of speaking. Such speech is certainly not referred to in total distinction from writing, since quotations of, and references to, texts in the Hebrew Bible (most quoted from the LXX) are common in Paul's writings and since he expected even his letters to be read aloud in assemblies of the church. First Thessalonians 5:27 expressly commands this, while the other letters seem to assume it. But the power of the spoken word appears to be paramount in Paul's understanding of gospel power.

Paul sees preaching as a vital link in the process of God's self-revelation and God's redemption of the whole of creation. The bottom line of the message is "Jesus Christ is Lord." The facts supporting that claim are the life, death, and resurrection of Jesus, facts that are announced along with the interpretation of their salvific significance. The continuing testimony in the word and life of the church validates the process.

Therefore, preaching presents God's view of reality in human language. When one is convinced (*pistis*) of the truth (*aletheia*) preached, one's whole mind-set is changed (*metanoia*: repentance; *phroneo kata pneuma*: minds set according to the spirit). This radical change Paul calls new creation, justification, peace with God, salvation, and redemption. This sort of total change could be effected only by divine power, so "for the apostle Paul preaching the gospel is the direct, vocal activity of the creative word of God in time and space."[15]

Our survey of other epistles, along with what we have already seen in earlier parts of the New Testament, indicate that Paul's position was not peculiar to him, but was consonant with the rest of the early church and to a great extent with the cultures in which he lived and worked.

---

[15]Beaudean, *Paul's Theology*, 192.

6

The Crux of the Gospel

Our cursory look at the New Testament in the preceding chapters indicates that the early church was convinced that the word that they were to shout from the housetops had been entrusted to them by the Lord himself and that its proclamation was empowered by the Lord to effect the salvation of humankind. We have also seen that references were made repetitively to the gospel, the word, or the proclamation as to a very specific message that so empowered. What was it? What is it?

What is the gospel we preach? That question invades seminary classes and ministerial meetings on a regular basis. It is a question that should be dealt with more often than it is and more seriously than is our usual approach. One could survey the use of the word *euangelion* (gospel) and its cognates through the New Testament. That would be a valuable discipline, especially if accompanied by a study of other words referring to communication and the content of early Christian communication, although for our present purposes we have done this sufficiently in earlier chapters.

The Cross of Christ

A broader view of the New Testament, however, leads us to a simple yet profound insight. A cursory reading of the four gospels impresses the reader with the overwhelming importance of the crucifixion and resurrection of Jesus. Not only the amount of space that each evangelist allots to the narration of those events but also the number of times that Jesus/both before and after his passion) is shown teaching about his death and resurrection, indicate the centrality of what Christians have always seen as God's primary salvific act.

In our survey of the gospel of Luke (chapter 3) I intentionally neglected the texts that focus on the crucifixion and resurrection of Jesus. Since those narratives grow out of the central proclamation of the early church, we cannot postpone any longer examining them. Not only do we find the vast bulk of the four gospels focused on the passion stories, but we see that each of the gospels leads up to those events by increasing the tension of the plot against Jesus and by increasing the frequency of Jesus' warning his disciples about what was coming. In Luke 19:41–44 we find the report of Jesus' weeping over Jerusalem and speaking words of deep foreboding. In Luke 20:27–40 we see Jesus giving the Sadducees more of an answer than they wanted to their question about marriage in a resurrection in which they refused to believe. Luke 21 is a chain of sayings of Jesus about the last days, which increases the sense of impending doom the way a master storyteller would.

Then Luke 22 combines the stories of the betrayal plans of Judas and the Last Supper with the disciples, followed by the retreat to Gethsemane and the arrest and trial of Jesus. Chapter 23 brings this to a climax with the trial before Pilate, the demand by the people for crucifixion, the *via dolorosa*, the crucifixion, and the burial.

This sequence of events is recorded by Luke in much the same way as it is in Matthew and Mark. A literary approach to origins sees this as evidence that Matthew and Luke were copied from Mark, but it has long been suggested that the earliest Christians told this part of the story of Jesus as an extended narrative from the earliest time.[1] The slight variations in detail from one gospel to the other are good indications that many different tellers were carrying this narrative. It is altogether possible that each of our four canonical gospels has recorded the telling of a different evangelist—a different teller of the good news.

---

[1]"Therefore, the Passion story must have been told from the very first in a specific order." Eduard Schweizer, *The Good News According to Mark*, trans. Donald H. Madvig (Atlanta: John Knox Press, 1970), 284f.

The verbal similarities that one finds in the gospel accounts of the passion stories (and in some instances the wording is identical) could be signs of the pressure of the early Christian communities to check the veracity of each telling. It is also most likely linked to use in the worship rituals of early churches. This is most obvious with (but not limited to) the narratives of the Last Supper. The early church told and retold these stories both within the community of faith and "from the housetops," so that by the time they were written down, they had been crafted by experts and worn smooth by use. The fact that such crafting and polishing seem to apply more to the passion narratives than to the rest of the gospel materials indicates that they formed the core of the teaching and preaching of the earliest church.

The sermons in Acts, no matter how they begin or progress, consistently bring their audiences to a confrontation with the death and resurrection of Jesus. Even the Areopagus sermon (Acts 17) ends with a reference to the man raised from the dead who will judge the world. Had the Areopagus sermon not been interrupted at that point, the unimpeded continuation of Paul's sermon would presumably have resembled his other mission sermons with the crucifixion and the resurrection. Thus, we see that the sermons in Acts offer even more evidence of the centrality of the cross and resurrection to the teaching and preaching of the early church.

The apostle Paul insists in his letters on returning to this formative moment in history as the crux (if you will excuse the Latin pun) of the gospel—the point of orientation for the Christian faith. The other New Testament epistles betray the same orientation. Even the book of Revelation repeatedly refers to Christ as the one who was slain and is alive. So everywhere we turn in the New Testament we see the crucifixion and resurrection of Jesus as the central fact of the good news and therefore as the primary content of the preaching and teaching of the first Christians.

The Resurrection of Christ

In contrast to the similarities among the accounts of the death of Jesus, each of our four gospels seems to treat the resurrection in its own way. Matthew (28:1–10) reports an earthquake and an angel whose appearance strikes fear in the hearts of the soldiers who were there, but who calms the fears of the women, who joyfully greet and worship the risen Lord. Mark (16:1–8), on the other hand, describes the women coming to the tomb and seeing a young man dressed in white, who tells them that Jesus has been raised and that they should take the news to his disciples and Peter.[2] Luke (24:1–49), in yet another version, reports on the women and then adds that Peter ran to check the empty tomb himself. He then details the story of the appearance to the Emmaus disciples, which leads him back to the other disciples in Jerusalem, where Jesus appears to the group, teaching and commissioning them. John (20:1–29) mentions only Mary Magdalene coming to find the tomb empty and going to tell Peter, who runs with the beloved disciple to investigate. After they leave, Mary remains and sees the risen Jesus, which she then announces (*angelousa*) to the gathered disciples. Later that day Jesus appears to them (minus Thomas) and a week later to the whole group. The appearance reported in John 21 forms a sort of epilogue to the book.

The only aspects of these narratives that are common to all four versions are the fact of the resurrection, testified to by the empty tomb and the initial visit of one or more women. The remainder of the details are put together by the evangelists (whether the final editors or earlier tellers) as complete and effective narratives, each of which must have been extremely important to a part of the community of faith.

The sermons in Acts and the epistles betray no attempt to narrate the details of the resurrection. We find there the proclamation that the crucified Jesus has been raised from the dead by the power of God for the salvation of human beings. As is made clear in Revelation, the crucifixion and the resurrection form one event, neither part of which is helpful by itself. "If Christ has not been raised" (1 Cor. 15:14), then the cross is but a symbol of a failed reformer. But since Christ has been raised, that fact stands as God's seal of approval both on the person and the work of Jesus and on the crucifixion as a redemptive event. Therefore, Paul can say what might very well have been a widely used confession of faith, that he "was handed over to death for our trespasses and was raised for our justification" (Rom. 4:25).

---

[2]According to the best textual scholarship, the other endings we have for Mark are likely later additions. For a helpful treatment of this see J. Lee Magness, *Sense and Absence: Structure and Suspension in the Ending of Mark's Gospel* (Atlanta: Scholars Press, 1986).

The Cross and the Christian Life

Another aspect of the thought of the early church concerning the Lord's passion is even more surprising. The implications of statements like the one by Paul, the great communicator of the gospel, in Galatians 2:19b–20 should challenge us: "I have been crucified with Christ; and it is no longer I who live, but it is Christ who lives in me." It is not just a question of why first-century Christians chose to center their lives on the death of their resurrected Lord. It is the continuing reality of that focus that makes the question ever relevant.

The Christian preacher is never able to escape the question, Why does the cross stand at the center of the gospel? The answer begins, of course, with the proclamation of the atoning death of Jesus on a cross. But as important as that is, the witness of the New Testament is not confined to the cross of Jesus. Nor is the testimony of the church so confined. We talk about the word of the cross. We sing about the way of the cross. We use the cross in church architecture, wear it as jewelry, and hang it on our walls. The cross seems to have something (at least symbolic) to do with how a Christian lives.

The disciple is one who takes up his or her cross daily to follow Jesus. Somehow in the experience of the early Christians the sacrificial death of Jesus was seen as introducing a whole new understanding and practice of human living to a world that, like ours, saw life in terms of personal prestige and power. The New Testament does not treat the cross as a once-and-done event, but as an event that has constant implications for the person whose life is touched by it. Whereas the way of the industrial-insurance complex is marked by self-justification, self-gratification, and self-preservation, the way of the cross is marked by self-denial. The woman or man whose life has been revolutionized by the one whom Jürgen Moltmann calls *The Crucified God*[3] will want to live the way of the cross.

The question remains, What does it mean to follow a risen Lord by bearing my own cross? For the early Christians it seems not to have meant imitating Jesus, but rather living a life appropriate for those for whom the cross of Christ is the single

---

[3]Jürgen Moltmann, *The Crucified God: The Cross of Christ as the Foundation and Criticism of Christian Theology*, trans. R. A. Wilson and John Bowden (New York: Harper & Row, 1974).

most important fact of history. That kind of discipleship is what Hans Küng called "the way of correlation—the way which is appropriate."[4] This seems to parallel the advice of the apostle Paul in Philippians 1:27, "Only, live your life in a manner worthy [*axios*] of the gospel of Christ." The word *axios* could better be translated "appropriate(ly)," as is true in its other New Testament appearances: Romans 16:2, Ephesians 4:1, Colossians 1:10, 1 Thessalonians 2:12, and 3 John 6. Except for the Romans passage, they all refer to the correlation of life with God, with the Lord, or with the Lord's calling. Since a central aspect of the gospel is humankind's inability to be worthy, the point is clearly that the Christian should form his or her life in a way appropriate to the gospel of the cross. In the words of Fred Craddock, those early witnesses "had adopted the cruciform life, 'always carrying in the body the death of Jesus' (II Corinthians 4:10)."[5]

On the basis of this analysis of the centrality of the cross in both the message and the life of the gospel, I offer the following seven statements for further reflection.

1. **Bearing my cross means to take sin as seriously as God does.** The Christian message of the mercy and grace of God, which is at the center of both the cross and the gospel, slips easily toward sentimentalism if it is not seen in the full dialectic of New Testament soteriology. Paul, in his epistle to the Romans, where he offers the fullest exposition we have of his doctrine of justification by grace through faith, guards against this slippage by beginning with (1:18—3:20) and returning to (5:12–21; 7:7–25) the reality and power of sin as the need of salvation and thus the reason for the cross.

The cross states loudly and clearly the fact that forgiveness is not easy, even for God. It informs us that God does not choose to be in the forgiveness business—that God would prefer to manage a world free of sin. Forgiveness is a risky business, a painful business. "You were bought with a price" (1 Cor. 6:20 and 7:23). "For our sake [God] made him to be sin who knew no sin, so that in him we might become the righteousness of God" (2 Cor. 5:21). The cross, which is an instrument of torture and death, cannot symbolize easy forgiveness or cheap grace. Alfred Lord Tennyson

---

[4]Hans Küng, *Christsein* (Münich: Deutscher Taschenbuch Verlag, 1974), 705 (au. trans.).
[5]Craddock, *Preaching* (Nashville: Abingdon Press, 1985), 59.

sensed this fact and put it in the mouth of King Arthur in his confrontation with his queen after her infidelity. She has prostrated herself before him, and along with his expressions of pain and wrath, she hears these words:

> Yet think not that I come to urge thy crimes;
> I did not come to curse thee, Guinevere,
> I, whose vast pity almost makes me die
> To see thee, laying there thy golden head,
> My pride in happier summers, at my feet.
> The wrath which forced my thoughts on that fierce law,
> The doom of treason and the flaming death—
> When I first learnt thee hidden here—is past.
> The pang—which, while I weig'd thy heart with one
> Too wholly true to dream untruth in thee,
> Made my tears burn—is also past—in part.
> And all is past, the sin is sinn'd, and I,
> Lo, I forgive thee, as Eternal God
> Forgives![6]

The Eternal God abhors sin, so that God's wrath must be revealed against it (Rom. 1:18), but God loves us human creatures, so much that divine grace is revealed to save us from his wrath. The cross—the symbol of the God-abandoned Son of God—shows how seriously God takes us and our sin. Thus, Paul and the other first-century Christian leaders reacted with shock to any hint of the attempted coexistence of sin and salvation. They recognized the continuing power of temptation but urged the rejection of sin by pointing out the absurdity and inappropriateness of continuing in sin. The most dangerous temptation of all for the believer appears to be the tendency to take lightly that which caused the death of Christ. The cross demands that we take sin seriously.

2. **Bearing my cross means to stay visible and vulnerable.** One can hardly hide a cross large enough to be hanged on, nor can one be hidden while carrying such a cross. We are so accustomed to seeing the beautiful and conveniently miniaturized representations of the cross that we tend to forget what a spectacle Jesus must have been on his *via dolorosa*—and how vulnerable.

---

[6]Alfred Lord Tennyson, "Guinevere," *Idylls of the King*, lines 529ff.

Vulnerability is a characteristic that we hesitate to attach to divinity. It implies risk, which seems to contradict characteristics like omnipotence and omniscience. And yet a casual reading of any of our New Testament gospels reveals Jesus repeatedly taking risks and being vulnerable. He was anything but careful, even in his choice of friends: the tax collectors, prostitutes, and revolutionaries. He even taught that his followers should free themselves from normal cares about even the necessities of life (Mt. 6:25–34).

But of course, the cross is the symbol of ultimate risk. "To lay down one's life for one's friends" (Jn. 15:13) is to be wholly vulnerable, for it is to practice unconditional love. And even the resurrection did not change this vulnerability. Having defeated death and being revealed now "with power" (Rom. 1:4), he did not bring the human race to its knees. He did not even "put the fear of God" into those who engineered and carried out his crucifixion. He graciously appeared to his disciples, allaying their fears, accommodating himself to their unbelief, assuaging their hunger, teaching, and finally giving them important work to do. This latter risk is perhaps the greatest of all, for in the commission, he entrusted to people like us the future of the life he died to give.

To match such visibility and vulnerability is a constant challenge to a follower of Jesus. To be salt and light is to be present and to be ready to lose everything in the service of others and of the Other.

3. **Bearing my cross means to be ready to suffer for the suffering.** If even God's Messiah found it necessary to be wounded in order to heal, his finite followers can hardly escape the same necessity. The realization of such a correlation must lie behind the words in Colossians 1:24, "I am now rejoicing in my sufferings for your sake, and in my flesh I am completing what is lacking in Christ's afflictions for the sake of his body, that is, the church."

Masochism does not seem to have been a natural part of Paul's psychological profile, but he was able to see a certain logic in his suffering as a follower of the crucified one. In fact, suffering for and suffering with people is not only to be expected in this world but is also very important for the rapport between communicator and receiver that is necessary for a true hearing of the gospel.

Furthermore, if Christ's purpose was to "create in himself one new humanity in place of the two, thus making peace, and [to] reconcile both groups to God in one body through the cross, thus putting to death that hostility through it" (Eph. 2:15b–16), then his followers in this one body should be working to reconcile the alien and the enemy to God and to God's people, fully expecting that such work will entail suffering.

4. **Bearing my cross means to risk life itself to resist the unjust.** Jesus was no doormat. To be visible and vulnerable does not necessarily mean allowing oneself to be trampled. He who did not run from controversy or even think twice about healing on the Sabbath is hardly glorified by disciples who pass by on the other side when they see a person in need. Jesus was crucified because he refused to conform to the unjust structures of his society. It is appropriate, then, that his followers should earn the reputation of being people who agitate the status quo (see Acts 17:6).

For the preacher to bring the gospel to bear on contemporary issues of justice and morals is an awesome task. One is always conscious of the danger of dividing a congregation over such issues. And yet in this age of increasing complexity and increasing speed of change, our hearers are hungry for help in sorting out the world in which they live. The increasing involvement of Christians in actions concerning peace and war, choice and abortion, free speech and pornography, and other burning issues indicates that our hearers are no longer satisfied with abstractions and generalities in the pulpit. The influence of preachers and preaching in the American civil rights movement should encourage preachers to study both the scriptures and the culture in order to speak the word of the gospel to real situations faced by real people every day.

5. **Bearing my cross means to do God's will in spite of cultural pressures.** The Gethsemane prayer of Jesus sets the scene for the cross. "Not what I want, but what you want" (Mk. 14:36; Mt. 26:39, 42; Lk. 22:42). The Sermon on the Mount, with its litany of "You have heard…, but I say" is, as John Stott recognized, a programmatic statement of a "Christian counter-culture."[7] On the basis of the gospel of the cross borne by that preacher, modern preachers who

---

[7]John R. W. Stott, *Christian Counter-Culture: The Message of the Sermon on the Mount* (Downers Grove, Ill.: InterVarsity Press, 1978).

trace their lineage back to him can but build a life centered on the will of God, no matter what our age demands of us. This is surely what Paul meant when he wrote, "Do not be conformed to this world [*aeon*], but be transformed by the renewing of your minds, so that you may discern what is the will of God—what is good and acceptable and perfect." (Rom. 12:2)

There is an old Russian proverb that reflects too well the attitude of most people of our age: "If given, grasp; if beaten, run fast."[8] To compare that with Jesus' teaching "But if anyone strikes you on the right cheek, turn the other also; and if anyone wants to sue you and take your coat, give your cloak as well" (Mt. 5:39–40) is to understand (whether or not one acts on that understanding) that God's will is rarely found in human culture.

The preacher striving to speak God's word to (and often against) a culture whose institutions and prevailing mores make it extremely difficult for Christians to emulate the Sermon on the Mount is bound to be in conflict with that culture and its institutions. But it is too easy for the church to become part of the environment and for its preaching merely to reflect the prevailing attitudes of its surroundings. The gospel of Christ wants to awaken its communicators so that they will speak boldly the word of grace in a context of greed.

6. **Bearing my cross means to live boldly, knowing that I am forgiven.** With all this discussion of the demand that the gospel be put into action, we are in danger of forgetting that it is, after all, a gospel of grace. That is what makes it good news. God's love for us is not conditioned on our goodness or our worthiness. It is said that when Philip Melanchthon was wrestling scrupulously with his own guilt, Luther's advice to him was, "*pecca fortiter*, 'Sin for all you are worth. God can forgive only a lusty sinner'"[9] Luther, of course, knew Melanchthon well enough to know that there was little danger of his becoming evil. But there was a real danger of his being paralyzed by a guilty conscience.

As a preacher becomes more and more conscious of the demands of the gospel, she or he should be reminded that at the

---

[8]John Barron, "Who Really Rules Russia?" *Readers Digest* (August 1985): 116.
[9]Roland Bainton, *Here I Stand* (New York: New American Library, 1950), 175.

heart of the gospel is forgiveness. If Peter had waited until his life was in total order before preaching, the world would never have heard his Pentecost sermon. Instead of focusing on his failures, he was able to find confidence in Christ's forgiveness and thus to preach boldly.

The cross, which is "the crux of the gospel," is not ours but Christ's. His cross means that we are forgiven. The cross that the Christian is to bear is not just another burden laid upon us by a harsh master; it symbolizes our release and continual freedom from the burden of guilt (Rom. 6:1–14; Col. 2:13–14).

7. **Bearing my cross means to face the future victoriously, knowing that nothing can overcome those who trust the crucified, living Lord.** One of the ironies of the history of the gospel is that the cross, the symbol of a cruel death, is the symbol of victory for the Christian. This is true because if death is no threat to us (1 Cor. 15:55–57), then we need fear nothing (Rom. 8:31–39). Such hope, which makes life livable and even enjoyable, is at the heart of the good news because of the cross. And therefore cross-bearing is not the resignation that tolerates the difficulties other people cause. It is creative. It is active. It is redemptive. It is a life of service.

Such a transformation of a leader's hideous death into a powerful symbol of life and victory can be understood only in light of the profound belief of those early Christians in the resurrection of Jesus from the dead. His victory over death made possible their expectation of sharing that victory in spite of the deathlike existence many of them faced. The death of Jesus became a point of orientation and the cross a symbol of victory through the power unleashed among believers by the resurrection of their Lord. Thus, even though some New Testament texts seem to emphasize the crucifixion at the expense of the resurrection, while a few (such as 1 Cor. 15:3ff.) seem to place the weight on the resurrection, the overwhelming impression left to the reader of these texts is that the two events are seen as inseparable—as really one climactic event in human history.

"*Crux probat omnia*," said Martin Luther.[10] The cross is always a test, even and especially of faith, since its explicit symbolism

---

[10]Martin Luther, *D. Martin Luther's Werke: Kritische Gesamtausgabe* (Weimar: H. Böhlau, 1883), 31, 179.

signifies weakness, disintegration, filth, and failure; but as a Christian symbol it signifies power, community, cleansing, and victory. The cross is also part of the gospel story, which is good news precisely because we can enter it. What William Bausch states about the resurrection is true also for the cross: "What counts are the implications the resurrection story has for us in our living and in sustaining our outlook on life and death. Otherwise you have reportage, not gospel."[11]

What is the gospel we preach? It is the good news of the cross— the cross Jesus bore, the cross that bore Jesus, the cross we bear daily. It is the good news that Jesus who died on that cross is alive. The combination of those two aspects of the faith transforms this message from a report of historical events to the world-changing promise of God to the human race. Peter's Pentecost sermon attaches the term "promise" to his proclamation of the events (Acts 2:39), since the significance of those events for people was redemptive. Jesus was not just handed over to death and raised, but he "was handed over to death for our trespasses and was raised for our justification" (Rom. 4:25). The implications of the gospel as promise will be investigated in chapter 7, after which we shall look at our contemporary preaching and hearing situation. For now, let us remember that the gospel we preach is the gospel we live in our cruciform lives, or it is no gospel at all.

Conclusion

It would have made even less sense in the first century than it does today to make a clear distinction between the content of a message and its intent and the methods used to communicate it. Since the heart of the gospel was and is the crucified and risen Lord Jesus Christ, the methods available to the early church, as well as to us, for telling the story and explaining its significance were many and varied. Yet the story was spread across the Roman Empire with marvelous speed, and it was kept surprisingly intact in the process.

The story was not just a recital of historical events but also a structure of life into which people were formed. This means that communication happened not just with words but also with the

---

[11]William Bausch, *Storytelling: Imagination and Faith* (Mystic, Conn.: Twenty-Third Publications, 1984), 196.

actions of those who said the words. Some of those speech acts took place in assemblies of believers and some in one-to-one acts of kindness, but they all communicated clearly to people who experienced them, as is recorded in summaries like Acts 2:47.

It remains for us to ask how following a crucified Master by living a life of personal sacrifice could have been so attractive to people even in the harsh world of the first-century Roman Empire. To attempt to comprehend this, our next chapter will look beyond the content of the message to its nature as a communication event.

7

The Gospel as Performative Speech

In our last chapter we discussed what we refer to as the content of the gospel—the significance of the crucifixion and resurrection of Jesus. Such a discussion is not unusual. A great deal of the energy of theologians during the Christian centuries has been devoted to defining and applying the meaning of the Christian gospel. Meaning is normally defined in terms of sense and referent, sense dealing with the significance of words and grammar and referent dealing with the historical veracity of the statements contained in the gospel. This process continues, as it should, with preachers and academics defining words, describing forms, and searching for historical connections.

Much more rarely do we ask about the *function* of Christian proclamation. In fact, I find that most preachers fail to have a clear idea of the intended function of individual sermons. We discuss our message. We assess our results. It is time for us to ask, Just what kind of communication of this specific message produces these specific results? We have seen that Paul attributes salvation to the utterance of this gospel (1 Cor. 1:21). How does that message attract people to a life of risk and sacrifice? What kind of utterance is the gospel? Can we find a description of the way that language works that will help us answer these questions? If it is true, as natural scientists tell us, that there is nothing more practical than a good theory, perhaps we need to find the right theory. Let me offer a suggestion.

Speech Act Theory

In 1955, John L. Austin offered in the William James Lectures at Harvard University some insight into language that may be useful for our purposes. Those lectures, published as *How to Do Things with Words*,[1] dealt in fine detail with the function of language. He pointed out that an utterance can not only inform a hearer, but it can also perform an act. Examples such as "I pronounce that they are husband and wife" or "We find the defendant not guilty" or "I bet you the Steelers will win" show us that certain speech acts in fact do not so much convey information as they accomplish an act. They marry, they pass judgment, they establish a wager. Austin calls such utterances "performatives."

The speech acts called performatives are marked off as different not by grammar, syntax, or vocabulary. The same words and the same forms can also convey information, and thus they can function as what Austin called "constatives." For this reason it is very easy to overlook the fact that performatives function differently than general locutions. With a performative utterance one can name a baby, launch a ship, establish a contract, effect a warning, or seal a promise. These are actions beyond the mere conveying of information. I maintain that the gospel of Christ is just this sort of speech act. Therefore, it is important for us to deal a bit more with speech act theory.[2]

To recognize a performative we need to look at it in its total context.[3] In order to actually perform something, an utterance must conform to understood cultural conventions. If the person who says, "I declare that they are husband and wife" is not authorized to perform a wedding or is not doing so at the time of the utterance, or if the man and woman do not have a valid marriage certificate, then the utterance performs nothing. It is what

---

[1]John L. Austin, *How to Do Things with Words*, 2d ed., ed. J. O. Urmson and Marina Sbisà, (Cambridge, Mass.: Harvard University Press, 1975).

[2]See also Austin's "Performative Utterances," in his *Philosophical Papers*, ed. J. O. Urmson and G. J. Warnock (Oxford: Clarendon Press, 1970), 233–52; his "Performative-Constative," in *The Philosophy of Language*, ed. John R. Searle (London: Oxford University Press, 1971), 13–22; and Sandy Petrey, *Speech Acts and Literary Theory* (New York: Routledge, 1990).

[3]Austin, *How to Do Things with Words*, 148: "The total speech act in the total speech situation is the *only actual* phenomenon which, in the last resort, we are engaged in elucidating" (emphasis in the original).

Austin calls "unhappy" or "infelicitous." True and false are not appropriate criteria in such a case. The act is either performed or it is not; the speech act is either happy/felicitous or it is not; it either does what it is intended to do or it is just so much sound or text.

In order for a performative statement to be happy, three conditions must be operative. First, the speaker must either *be* the person authorized to perform the act, or the speaker must refer somehow to the proper authority. Second, the speech act must be understood by the hearer(s) as it is intended by the speaker. There must be some cultural convention in operation; for example, the culture must accept that this is a wedding ceremony and that these words uttered by this authorized person seal the marriage. And third, the utterance and its accompanying convention "must be executed by all participants both correctly and completely."[4] For instance, if a wedding ceremony is performed as part of a theater performance, it is understood that it is not a valid ceremony— that the words do not accomplish what they would if these three conditions were operative.

The Gospel as Speech Act

Just how does the gospel fit into this scheme of language? What kind of performative speech act is the proclamation of the gospel? A number of New Testament texts indicate that the gospel is a promise, which we noted above is a specific type of performative utterance. Toward the close of the report of Peter's Pentecost sermon in Acts 2, we find an explicit statement to this effect. Peter has put his sermon in the framework of Hebrew prophecy by quoting and commenting on Joel 2:28–32, Psalm 16:8–11, and Psalm 110:1 and by referring to other prophetic texts. In this way he has called forth a cultural convention in which Jewish people would expect to hear a declaration of God's intention for them, in the form of either a warning or a promise. With direct reference to these texts, the preacher tells about the death and resurrection of Jesus of Nazareth and his resultant establishment as Lord and Messiah. In response to the frantic question of his hearers, "What should we do?" Peter replies (v. 38), "Repent, and be baptized every one of you in the name of Jesus Christ so that your sins may be forgiven; and you will receive the gift of the

---

[4]Austin, *How to Do Things with Words*, 14–15.

Holy Spirit." He then continues (v. 39) with the words, "For the promise [*he epangelia*] is for you, for your children, and for all who are far away, everyone whom the Lord our God calls to him." Here is Simon Peter, a close associate of the risen and exalted Lord, in a context of Hebrew prophecy, uttering God's promise that the repentant one who is baptized will be forgiven and will receive the Holy Spirit. This is an audacious utterance, but it appears that in that context, many of those hearers were convinced that they were hearing from God himself. The miracle of tongues, which had been the occasion of the speech, and Peter's connecting it with the coming of God's Spirit established Peter as one who could speak for God. Therefore, Peter's references to what God was promising could be received by the people at face value. The report concludes (v. 41), "So those who welcomed his message were baptized, and that day about three thousand persons were added."

It seems helpful to note here that Austin classifies a promise in the class of performatives he labels "commissives."[5] A commissive commits the speaker or, in this case, the God represented by the speaker to do something. Thus, the utterance of the gospel can be seen as the giving of God's commitment to forgive and support the hearers, while the reception of the promise by the hearers in faith is their acceptance of that promise as coming from the God who is able to perform it.

This construction of the gospel as promise does not appear to be an invention of Peter's, since both Matthew and Mark record quite similar words from Jesus himself. Mark has it (and Matthew 4:17 is not radically different), "Now after John was arrested, Jesus came to Galilee, proclaiming the good news [gospel] of God, and saying, 'The time is fulfilled, and the kingdom of God has come near; repent, and believe in the good news'" (1:14–15). Surely those Galileans would have heard such a statement as the restatement and assurance of the imminent fulfillment of God's ancient promise.

The Gospel as Promise in Paul

Paul, in both Romans 4 and Galatians 3, brings together the concepts of gospel and promise. The apostle sets up his use of Abraham in Romans 4 by declaring in the preceding chapter (3:27ff.) that God is God of both Jews and Gentiles, since all are

---

[5]Ibid., 151–52.

justified on the basis of faith. He then chooses to draw his primary example for such faith from Abraham. In the process of the argument, Paul refers to God as both Judge (in those days the only person who could justify) and Creator. In Paul's mind both justification and creation would be verbal acts. The verdictive, "I find you not guilty," is the act of justification. Furthermore, the ancient faith of the Hebrews that God created all that exists by his word of command is a prime example of a performative utterance. We find Paul making that very connection explicit in 2 Corinthians 4:6, "For it is the God who said, 'Let light shine out of darkness,' who has shone in our hearts to give the light of the knowledge of the glory of God in the face of Jesus Christ." God's utterance causes things to happen!

Therefore, when Paul identifies God as the one "who justifies the ungodly" (Rom. 4:5), as well as the one "who gives life to the dead and calls into existence the things that do not exist" (v. 17), he is identifying God as the one whose speech performs wonders. We should also note that God's calling is connected in the Old Testament with the exodus from Egypt and other divine acts of redemption. This is made clear in Hosea 11:1–2, "When Israel was a child, I loved him, and out of Egypt I called my son. The more I called them, the more they went from me; they kept sacrificing to the Baals, and offering incense to idols." The call, the sound of God's voice, the word of the Lord—these are all designations in the Hebrew Bible of God's power to perform.

Pointing, then, to that authority, universally recognized by Jews and the God-fearers who constituted the majority of the earliest Christians, Paul goes on to tell us (v. 20f.) that Abraham trusted the promise he had received from God because he was fully convinced that God was able to *do* what he had promised. Paul then connects this God who promises with the actual content of the gospel when he adds one more identifying statement about God, that he is the one "who raised Jesus our Lord from the dead," which he follows up with an early version of the basic confession of Christian faith, "who was handed over to death for our trespasses and was raised for our justification" (vv. 24–25).

In Galatians 3:6–9, Paul connects Christian faith with the belief of Abraham, going so far as to say that the scripture report of Abraham's faith and God's promise (Gen. 15:6 and 12:3) "declared the gospel beforehand" (*proeuangelisato*). The promise to Abraham, "All the Gentiles shall be blessed in you," is being fulfilled in

Christians. Paul then reminds his readers in verses 10–14 of the curse of the law, which functions here as the negative side of the promise. This paragraph closes with the words "so that we might receive the promise of the Spirit through faith" (v. 14b). Paul continues to contrast the law and its curse with the promise that comes to faith, although he flatly denies (v. 21) that the law was "opposed to the promises of God." Paul firmly believed that "God is one" (v. 20). This ancient (*shema*) statement of the faith of Israel kept Paul in his search for ways to communicate the Torah as God's word and the gospel as God's promise. He was led to see the law also as promise, in the sense that it looked forward to the gospel. "Therefore the law was our disciplinarian until Christ came, so that we might be justified by faith" (Gal. 3:24). Here the NRSV translates *paidagogos* as "disciplinarian" to indicate accurately that the law was not so much a teacher as a servant whose responsibility it was to prepare pupils for the coming teacher. Thus, Paul in this text employs *epangelia* (promise) as a synonym of *euangelion* (gospel) with a firm sense of continuity with the promises of God to the Israelites.

In addition to the multiple connections with promise in Galatians 3, we find an exceptionally clear summary statement in Ephesians 3:6, "the Gentiles have become fellow heirs, members of the same body, and sharers in the promise in Christ Jesus through the gospel." This sentence ends a paragraph in which Paul uses the term *mystery* several times in reference to the revelation he was communicating. Mystery here is something already revealed in Christ, so Paul appears to mean by it the strategy that God had been using to prepare for the communication of the divine promise to all people through Israel. Even though God had made this promise of universal blessing clear to Abraham, it had become a mystery to many of Abraham's descendants until the advent of Christ. The promise had always been operative; it had become hidden during that intervening period of human history. The gospel reveals what was for a time a mystery—it communicates the divine promise.

It should then be no surprise that Paul's sermon in the synagogue in Antioch of Pisidia, as it is reported in Acts 13:16ff., also makes the connection between prophecy and promise. After setting the stage with a summary of the history of God's dealing faithfully with unfaithful Israel, he declares the resurrected Jesus.

In making this crucial turn, he says, "And we bring you the good news that what God promised to our ancestors he has fulfilled for us, their children, by raising Jesus" (v. 32–33a). Then after quoting Psalm 2:7, Isaiah 55:3, and Psalm 16:10 and after referring to David's story in 1 Kings 2:10, Luke reports that Paul ends the sermon with an exhortation to action, using Habakkuk 1:5. His penultimate utterance is, "Let it be known to you therefore, my brothers, that through this man forgiveness of sins is proclaimed to you; by this Jesus everyone who believes is set free from all those sins from which you could not be freed by the law of Moses" (vv. 38–39). This certainly has the characteristics of a promise renewed as the fulfillment of a promise.

The Content of the Promise

The preaching and teaching of the early church dealt often and sometimes extensively with the gospel of Christ as the fulfillment of God's promise mediated through the Hebrew prophets. Thus, one aspect of the meaning of gospel as promise is its history. God has shown through the history of Israel that divine promises can be trusted. God keeps God's word.

The specific promise conveyed by the preaching of the gospel appears to have been the forgiveness of sin. Acts 2:38–39; 3:19–20; 5:31; 10:43; and 13:38–39 record the promise of forgiveness in four of the main apostolic sermons in the book of Acts. In others, forgiveness is alluded to by the term *salvation* (4:12; 16:30–31). The exceptions are Stephen's sermon (chapter 7) and Paul's Areopagus sermon (17:22–34), both of which are reported as having been interrupted before they were finished.

Other aspects of the promise can be seen in connection with forgiveness. Eternal life is contingent on forgiveness, since it means being in the presence of the holy God. Justification, reconciliation, atonement, redemption, and peace with God are all terms from various semantic domains that in the New Testament refer to some facet of forgiveness. The inclusion of the Gentiles in God's reign is a major concern of Paul, and it is another way of talking about the forgiveness of sin being offered not only to Jews, but also to the rest of the human race. In short, the promise of the gospel is God's offer of a way out of the human predicament we call sin— a way made possible by the grace of God in the crucified and risen Lord Jesus Christ.

Conclusion

It seems clear that Paul and Luke, like Peter, expected the *euangelion* (gospel) to function as the ultimate fulfillment of the *epangelia* (promise) of God down through history. The gospel did not replace the promise, but rather it was both that to which the promise had referred and a new and ultimate promise in its own right. Even in 1 Corinthians 15:3–8, to which we referred earlier as an example of a logical presentation of the content of the gospel, it is clear that the gospel consists of more than historical information (Jesus died, was buried, and was raised). It includes also what has been referred to as interpretation, but which might better be understood as promise: "for our sins in accordance with the scriptures."

As Austin points out,[6] to be "happy," a performative speech act needs complete and correct execution by all participants. If we apply this criterion to the preaching of the gospel, we can see that what is lacking in the transaction of this promise is the conviction (*pistis*: faith) of the receiver(s). Paul puts all this together in a text to which we continue to return, Romans 10:17: "So conviction (*pistis*) comes out of a hearing (*akoe*), and the hearing comes through the utterance (*rhema*) of Christ."[7] According to Romans 4, Abraham's faith allowed God's promise to operate (Sarah's womb to bear!); in Romans 10 in like manner Paul summarizes the salvation process (this time referring to Moses, in vv. 5–8) in terms of a complete speech transaction. Proclamation of this gospel results in the confession of Jesus as Lord. And according to 10:17 the means of it all is the word of Christ (*dia rhematos Christou*). If Paul intended to refer here to a message about Christ, he would have more naturally used the term *logos*. But if what Paul has in mind with the utterance of the message is that God effects a transaction through the preaching, then *rhema Christou* here must signify the hearing of this preaching as hearing the very utterance of Christ, who, as Lord, has the authority to make a promise of divine forgiveness. In addition, Paul's earlier reference (v. 16) to Isaiah's use of the same word establishes the connection with the history of God's promise through the prophets.

---

[6]Ibid., 15.
[7]Author's translation.

So here we have the requisites complete. Christ is authorized to speak the promise on behalf of God. He has been faithful to his mandate—faithful even to death. The culture established between God and the people of Israel offers the convention of the divine promise. A speaker commissioned by God and empowered by God's spirit communicates the promise. Then the hearer is convinced by the words of God's representative, thus accepting the promise. It now remains for us to deal with the implications of this understanding of the gospel for our contemporary preaching.

How can we, with our contemporary cultural conventions (what the scholars of orality call "communication registers") utter the gospel in such a way that people will hear it as God's promise? This question should always be in our minds as we prepare to preach. There can be no timeless or universal answer to such a question, since cultural conventions differ from time to time and from place to place. However, we might be able to state some helpful guidelines. Therefore, our next chapter will attempt to analyze the way people today tend to listen. This study should give us some guidance regarding the best way to prepare to preach.

8

Truth in Love: The Congregation as Context

The assembled congregation composes the environment or context of most preaching in the Western world today. We can readily see that although preaching took place in the assemblies of the first-century church, most of the preaching recorded in the book of Acts was to unbelievers. This remains true in many parts of our world—parts we refer to as mission fields. In recent years missiologists have noted increasing similarities between those mission fields and the cultures of Europe and North America. Thus, we would be well advised to begin thinking again about preaching to unbelievers.[1]

However, in this chapter we shall look at the congregation as the primary context for preaching. We have noted above (chapter 2) that in primarily oral cultures the audience was the guarantor of the integrity of the story, since stories were customarily repeated often. Those audiences were pleased by a good retelling of the traditional stories; they were not as interested in originality as we are. A similar situation exists in the church today, increased to some extent by our easy access to the written gospel. The core of the Christian story we expect to remain the same. The details of

---

[1]A beginning in this direction has been made by William Willimon in *The Intrusive Word: Preaching to the Unbaptized* (Grand Rapids, Mich.: Eerdmans, 1994).

its telling and the applications of its significance to our lives are open to creativity.

Therefore, we look now at the role of the congregation of Christians as the primary hearers of Christian preaching. One could certainly argue that the unconverted should be the ones hearing the gospel, and we should be aware of seekers in our services, as well as regular attendees who still need to be converted. However, in the present work we are looking at the status quo, not the ideal. Also, we have the reminder in Acts 20:7–12 that early congregations received apostolic communication. Knowing then that believers, as well as unbelievers, need to be addressed by the gospel, we turn, fittingly, to a New Testament passage that can help believers become a receptive context for the hearing of the word.

Ephesians 4:15

Ephesians 4:15 is only a small part of a single sentence that comprises verses 11–16:

> The gifts he gave were that some would be apostles, some prophets, some evangelists, some pastors and teachers, to equip the saints for the work of ministry, for building up the body of Christ, until all of us come to the unity of the faith and of the knowledge of the Son of God, to maturity, to the measure of the full stature of Christ. We must no longer be children, tossed to and fro and blown about by every wind of doctrine, by people's trickery, by their craftiness in deceitful scheming. But speaking the truth in love, we must grow up in every way into him who is the head, into Christ, from whom the whole body, joined and knit together by every ligament with which it is equipped, as each part is working properly, promotes the body's growth in building itself up in love.

This context defines the point of reference and the connections of the two terms, which are the central focus of our present investigation. The author's[2] major concern here is the church: its

---

[2]Scholars are divided over the authorship of Ephesians, many of them pointing to differences of style, vocabulary, and emphasis from the undisputedly Pauline letters. I tend to agree with Markus Barth in his *Ephesians*, vol. 34, *The Anchor Bible* (Garden City, N.Y.: Doubleday, 1974), 41, who, having fully reviewed the evidence, concludes, "Although it cannot be definitely proved that Ephesians is genuinely Pauline, nevertheless it is still possible to uphold its authenticity."

unity, its ministry, and the leadership necessary to the maintenance of unity and the praxis of ministry. Here in verses 11–12 he first lists the Lord's gifts of leadership ministers (apostles, prophets, evangelists, pastors, and teachers). We noted earlier that all of these functions include oral communication. He then lists their divine purpose ("to equip the saints for the work of ministry, for building up the body of Christ"). Verse 13 states the goal of God for all Christians (the attaining of "the unity of the faith and of the knowledge of the Son of God," i.e., "to maturity, to the measure of the full stature of Christ"). Verse 14 then describes the alternative to such growth (being "children, tossed to and fro and blown about by every wind of doctrine"). Verses 15 and 16 state the positive expected result (growing up and being built up in love). The four words in the original text that stand between these negative and positive statements are our focus of attention in this chapter: *aletheuontes de en agape.*

Since the English language has no verbal form of the word *truth,* as does Greek, a translator of this phrase is compelled either to coin a term ("truthing"?) or to import a verb ("speaking the truth" or "doing the truth"). I suggest that if we consider carefully the connection between truth and love shown in this passage, we can paraphrase the problematic words to translate their meaning more fully than we can by means of either of the two usual options.

"In love" describes a context or environment for whatever the author means by "truthing." Moreover, the whole situation is set forth here as the necessary circumstance for the growth that is the expected result of the ministry of the united church. There appears to be no basis in the New Testament for our penchant toward distinguishing between numerical and spiritual growth. The summary reports in the book of Acts indicate that as believers grew in their piety and concern for one another, the number of believers also increased. Thus, whether or not preaching was done in the assembly of believers, much of the early church's preaching could call upon the quality of life in the church as the hearers' context. It seems obvious, therefore, that the context referred to in Ephesians 4 by the phrase "in love" is the church itself. We are dealing with ministry (including preaching) within and to the church.

As we all know, the truth can be spoken outside the context of a loving community of faith. In fact, if evangelism is to take place, the truth of the gospel must be spoken outside the faith community, although as I indicated above, the speaker can refer to the community as the environment and exhibition of the gospel. In addition, we must confess with shame that truth can be spoken with little of the warmth of love. We may question whether the gospel can be communicated without love, but we must admit that true statements can be spoken or written about it without love. Thus, our author must have had more in mind here than just speaking the truth of the gospel.

What sort of experience or event could be referred to by "truthing in love?" The present participle indicates action and not just words.[3] To do the truth must mean at least to be honest or open about oneself. This kind of vulnerability is especially important, and under normal circumstances possible only, in a tolerant (loving) group.

In fact, such truthing and such love are mutually dependent. Unless one is driven to desperation, one can hardly be honest about one's deepest feelings in a group that is not loving. We must be assured of tolerance and unconditional acceptance before we can completely trust another individual or others in a group. The kind of unselfish love (*agape*) that is unconditionally accepting of another person is precisely the identifying mark of Christian relationships (see Jn. 13:35). In order to restore such tolerance in the church at Rome, Paul wrote (Rom. 15:7): "Welcome one another, therefore, just as Christ has welcomed you, for the glory of God." So it should be in the church, as in no other community, where a person will be accepted just as she or he is.

Therefore, it is in the church ("in love") where truth can be demonstrated—where one can be totally honest, without fear of rejection or betrayal. Doing the truth in this way, then, can happen only in such an environment of love. But I said truth and love are *mutually* dependent. How is love dependent on honesty? Even if we have not experienced it for ourselves, we have all seen in others how dishonesty or defensiveness erodes love. Too often relationships are broken because one or both persons refuse to communicate on all levels. Such reserve often creates barriers that the strongest love from another cannot break through.

So love is the environment in which truth can be lived, and openness is the element that keeps the love vital. The ministry of

---

[3]See T. K. Abbott, *The Epistles to the Ephesians and Colossians*, International Critical Commentary (Edinburgh: T. & T. Clark, 1977), 123: "Verbs in -euo express the doing of the action which is signified by the corresponding substantive in -eia."

the word (note again the oral functions of the list in Eph. 4:11) should both contribute to and profit from the development of the kind of open tolerance, or tolerant openness, described by our Ephesians text. Both the members of our congregations and the unbelievers we contact are attracted to such authentic relationships and open communication. So being truthful in the context of accepting love should lead to the extremely satisfying kind of personal and corporate growth described in verses 15 and 16.

Can We Do It?

But accomplishing this goal is harder than talking about it. Reinhold Niebuhr reflected on the problem in 1924:

> I am not surprised that most prophets are itinerants. Critics of the church think we preachers are afraid to tell the truth because we are economically dependent upon the people of our church. There is something in that, but it does not quite get to the root of the matter. I certainly could easily enough get more money than I am securing now, and yet I catch myself weighing my words and gauging their possible effect upon this and that person. I think the real clue to the tameness of a preacher is the difficulty one finds in telling unpleasant truths to people whom one has learned to love.
>
> To speak the truth in love is a difficult, and sometimes an almost impossible, achievement. If you speak the truth unqualifiedly, that is usually because your ire has been aroused or because you have no personal attachment to the object of your strictures. Once personal contact has been established you are very prone to temper your wind to the shorn sheep. It is certainly difficult to be human and honest at the same time. I'm not surprised that most budding prophets are tamed in time to become harmless parish priests...
>
> What is satisfying about the ministry is to note how far you can go in unfolding the full meaning of the Christian gospel provided you don't present it with the implication that you have attained and are now laying it as an obligation upon others.
>
> If the Christian adventure is made a mutual search for truth in which the preacher is merely a leader among many

searchers and is conscious of the same difficulties in his [*sic*] own experience which he [*sic*] notes in others, I do not see why he [*sic*] cannot be a prophet without being forced into itinerancy.[4]

All preachers can very easily identify with the young Niebuhr's dilemma. It *is* "difficult to be human and honest at the same time." But we dare not back away from such a dilemma as though it were alien. In fact, the tension lies at the heart of the gospel; perhaps we can say it lies at the very heart of God. God chose, after all, to reveal God's nature and to offer humankind the hope of salvation because of divine love. And therefore, God's grace determined that the ultimate revelation should come not in unalterable statements of truth, but rather in the life of one who said, "I am...the truth" and, "As the Father has loved me, so I have loved you" (Jn. 14:6 and 15:9). The category of God's truth must be understood as absolute, but the communication of that truth by and through the person of Jesus the Christ is tempered with love. In fact, this divine love is so much a part of the revealed truth that scripture can claim that "God is love" (1 Jn. 4:8). Divine truth can never be relative truth, but at the same time truth that comes from the God who is love by means of the one who showed us what true love is can never be rigid. Nor should it ever be used to hurt, only to help.

Practicing openness in an environment of love sounds like an ideal toward which preaching should prod people. And so it is. But it is also a description of a reality close to the center of the gospel. God's self-revelation in the living word put God in the extremely vulnerable position of trusting creatures who had already demonstrated their (our?) untrustworthiness. And so it continues. God still entrusts that word of truth and love to human beings—to sinners. And we who live it and preach it know the experience of vulnerability that accompanies it. We also know the power. Love destroys barriers to hearing. Truth that is heard changes lives. Participation in the honest sharing of a loving community brings healing.

Therefore, we preach. Therefore, we willingly and regularly put ourselves in a position of vulnerability. Therefore, we take up the seemingly impossible task of communicating a word of the

---

[4]Reinhold Niebuhr, *Leaves from the Notebook of a Tamed Cynic* (San Francisco: Harper & Row, 1980), 53–54.

infinite God to the understanding of finite persons. When our love wears thin and when we are unsure of the love of our hearers, still "the love of Christ urges us on" (2 Cor. 5:14).

Truthing in love—being open to one another in an environment of love—describes a Christian community in which full communication is possible. But we are left with one problem: how to begin. For the most part, I'm afraid, people do not think of the church as a place where they can be totally honest about themselves. I made a presentation in one congregation on the importance of such vulnerability, and later I heard one woman speak very honestly in a small group. She first expressed how important it was for her to have a few good friends with whom she could confide her inmost thoughts and feelings, but then she confessed that the church is the last place she would expect to develop such relationships. Too often our services of worship, including our preaching, contribute more to hypocrisy than to openness. People are led to assume that when they have negative thoughts or feelings, there is something wrong with them—that real Christians should not be negative. They therefore are more apt to hide such thoughts than to confide them to the church. Whether or not we Christians do this intentionally, the fact is that it happens.

If being open depends on the assurance of love, and love grows with the stimulation of openness, getting started must be akin to boarding a moving carousel. It is risky business. Once again, we are faced with the necessity of vulnerability. Somebody must take the risk, and it should probably be the chief communicator—in this case, the preacher. Admitting such vulnerability is often harder for the pastor/preacher than for others. However, if the gospel of the cross really is God's power for salvation, the preacher of that gospel should be willing to run the risk of speaking without any personal authority except that of truth and love. Doing so would certainly change the structures of our preaching, but it would also bring the preaching into line with the essence of the gospel.

This leads us to the challenge facing the preacher at the beginning of the twenty-first century. People today are not so much interested in logical or authoritative truth as they are in authenticity as displayed in the life of a speaker and the relationships of the community that claims to believe the truth. Is this so different from the challenge that faced the primitive church? The summaries in Acts (2:43–47; 4:32–35; 5:12–16; 6:7; 9:31;

11:19–21; 12:24) indicate the close connection between the impression made by the church and the reception of the gospel preached by the apostles. We have used the terms *openness* and *vulnerable* in place of *truth* in Ephesians 4:15. Perhaps our postmodern paraphrase of "truthing in love" should be "communicating authenticity in an environment of love."

Conclusion

The gospel must be heard in order to effect faith (Rom. 10:17). So the hearer, as always, is a very important component of communication. The nature of the gospel makes the attitude of the assembled hearers even more important than in other communication situations. When this word, which refers to the truth of God revealed in the love of Christ, is spoken into a context of persons who revere the truth and love one another, great life-changing power is unleashed. The consistent testimony of the New Testament is that such a combination is the description of the church of Jesus Christ as it should be—an assembly of people open to the movement of God's spirit in and through the truth and love they share with one another. As we saw in chapter 2, the early church was a community that held the speaking of truth as a primary virtue. The words of Jesus in John 13:35, "By this everyone will know that you are my disciples, if you have love for one another," indicate the importance of love in the community of his followers. The two together prepare a people for powerful and power-releasing communication.

The combination of a prepared preacher and prepared hearers has always been important, but its importance appears to be increasing exponentially as the environment of communication changes. Most observers of the postmodern scene indicate that truth for the postmodern thinker is always tied to the community that claims or proclaims it. We often hear people say, "That might be true for you, but I don't see it that way." We can mourn the loss of absolute truth all we want, but we should also recognize the advantage we have of the truth set in a context of love. Acts 4:32–34 shows how the early church took advantage of this connection:

> Now the whole group of those who believed were of one heart and soul, and no one claimed private ownership of any possessions, but everything they owned was held in common. With great power the apostles gave their

testimony to the resurrection of the Lord Jesus, and great grace was upon them all. There was not a needy person among them, for as many as owned lands or houses sold them and brought the proceeds of what was sold.

The loving care of the church added power to the preaching of the truth by the apostles, the combination of which brought grace upon everyone.

How then should we prepare to preach? This question will be the focus of our attention in the next chapter.

9

Preparing to Preach
vs. Sermon Preparation

Most preachers have had one or more courses on sermon preparation. In such courses they have learned to choose and study a text or to define a topic; they have been prodded to describe an audience; and they have been shown how to formulate an oral presentation to that audience about the topic or text. Sometimes they have even been led to state an objective for the sermon. In most cases the courses have focused primarily on the task of the preacher in moving from a text or topic through an oral presentation.

But as we have seen, oral communication of the gospel of the cross should be more than the preparation of a twenty-minute argument and its delivery in a way that people can understand it. Because of the nature of the gospel, its communication is somehow both the self-expression of the speaker and the word of God. In addition, as we saw in the previous chapter, our hearers now demand "authenticity." For these reasons, we should consider carefully the preparation of the preacher whenever we deal with the preparation of sermons. In other words, we need to prepare not only a presentation but also a presenter. We should prepare to preach, not just to deliver a sermon.

The Preacher and God

Preparing the preacher to preach God's word effectively to God's people necessarily involves making sure that the preacher is God's speaker. As we noted in chapter 2, the early Christians spoke in the consciousness that they had a commission from the Son of God himself. In chapter 7 we noted that the communication of the gospel as God's promise depends in part on the perception of the hearers that the preacher is speaking on behalf of God. Since biblical times we have talked about "the call to preach," understanding this to mean that we are somehow commissioned by God as messengers of the divine word.

Such a commission should not be taken for granted. What is true for all Christians in this regard must be taken especially seriously by those of us who are called to be preachers. We must live in the disciplines that will enliven and deepen our relationship with God. It is not my purpose here to give instruction in the spiritual disciplines—only to admonish myself and others to pray, meditate, worship, and study regularly so that we keep open the lines of communication with God. We should do whatever it takes to see to it that, in the words of Paul, "after proclaiming to others I myself should not be disqualified" (1 Cor. 9:27).

Some people are self-disciplined enough to maintain a vital program of spiritual growth on their own. However, many of us need constant prodding. This kind of help can be found in relationships of accountability with another person or a group. Such people can be found among area ministers or within a local congregation of Christians. Whoever we find and however we structure this support, a covenant of mutual accountability and encouragement can be a decisive factor in our spiritual maintenance programs.

Because most preachers also plan, prepare, and lead the worship assemblies of the churches they serve, they find it difficult to enter fully into corporate worship. Numerous times I have been told by preachers that they find it impossible to worship. This is more than regrettable. It probably contributes to the discouragingly high burnout rate among preachers. We should recognize that we can offer to God our preparation time for both worship and preaching as an act of worship. We should also increase our awareness that the sermon in the context of corporate worship is itself worship. As we encourage others to present themselves and their work to God in worship, so we preachers can present to God ourselves and our work of preaching and leading worship. If attention to details makes this difficult, it is time to turn the details over to others so that they do not interfere with our worship. During a brief visit to Korea, I was impressed with the custom of preachers of kneeling in prayer prior to seating themselves before the congregation. I discovered that this helped me to concentrate on God during the service, and I assume that it reminded the rest of the congregation that we preachers went about God's business in a special yet worshipful way.

The Preacher and God's People

In addition to guarding our relationship with God, it is vital that we maintain good relationships with God's people. The preacher is not a freestanding fountain of divine wisdom, but is part of a line of faithful witnesses that stretches back over two thousand years and outward into all the world.

For this reason we can find much important help in the experiences of God's messengers throughout history. The lives of the patriarchs and the Hebrew prophets, the examples of the apostles and Christian prophets, the models found among the church fathers and missionaries, the stories of the reformers, the more familiar biographies of recent preachers—all of these work to remind us of where we came from and who we are. They show us that the challenges we face are, for the most part, not new. They encourage us with the knowledge that those challenges have been survived and even overcome by women and men who were "more than conquerors through him who loved us" (Rom. 8:37).

Not only are we a part of a stream of tradition; we are also participants in a global community. It would be helpful if every preacher could travel around the world for a year to visit Christians in various cultures who are faithfully communicating the gospel. Since this is hardly possible, we should take opportunities offered us to hear and read about Christians in other lands. We should become acquainted with international Christians who are studying or working temporarily in our vicinities. Such people can teach us a great deal about faith and spirituality, and our contacts with them, however fleeting, can give us insight into the reality of Christ's universal church.

We are also part of a fellowship of preachers close to home. Whether through an organization or through personal contacts, it is important for preachers to know that there are others called by God who are working generally the same field. Just as student preachers give one another stimulation and encouragement in a seminary classroom or student lounge, preachers away from such opportunities can find or create similar experiences. I am aware of groups of preachers meeting each week to discuss the text from which they will all be preaching on the next Sunday. I know of other cases where this is done by telephone or e-mail. This sort of fellowship reminds us that we are not alone in our calling and its attendant responsibilities.

Perhaps more pressing than any of these issues is the need to relate appropriately to the congregation to which we preach. In chapter 8, we have already discussed the ideal nature of the congregation in terms of truth and love. Now it is important to remind ourselves that we are members of congregations. Tom Long has reflected in a helpful way on the multifaceted relationship between preacher and congregation. In his discussion of images of the preacher, he deals with the herald, the pastor, the storyteller, and finally the witness. Under that category he states:

> Accordingly, the church prepares and trains its ministers, including sending them to seminaries, not because ministers are better or smarter than other Christians, but because the church needs workers equipped to help the church to know the truth and to live in its light. If the preacher is to be the one sent to listen for God's truth in the Bible, the preacher not only must be willing to listen to the Bible but also must know how to listen. If the preacher is to be sent on behalf of the congregation, the preacher must also know how to listen to *them*.[1]

Much recent homiletical discussion has focused on the nature of preaching as conversation. By this we do not mean that it is spoken in a calm, "conversational" tone, but rather that a sermon is part of an ongoing conversation between a preacher and a congregation.[2] Such a conversation can be used directly in the development of sermons if the preacher is willing to invite other members of the congregation into the preparation process.

---

[1]Thomas G. Long, *The Witness of Preaching* (Louisville: Westminster/John Knox Press, 1989), 44. Emphasis is in the original.

[2]For a good summary, see John S. McClure, "Conversation and Proclamation: Resources and Issues," *Homiletic* 22, no. 1 (Summer 1997), 1–13.

Initiating this sort of group process can be intimidating, but we who have tried it will testify that the development of a group of people within the congregation who are directly involved in the thought process that produces the sermon will enliven both the preaching and the hearing of it.[3] Those people grow to appreciate the demanding task of sermon preparation, and they can also be enlisted to pray for the preacher through the process of preparation and preaching. They thus become not only assistants in the task of preaching, but also supporters and the finest of listeners. They will be the first to understand that proclamation of the gospel is the responsibility of the whole church, not just of a chosen few.

General congregational relationships and pastoral work are also of vital importance to the preaching ministry. I was once told that Harry Emerson Fosdick was given the "privilege" early in his ministry at Riverside Church to concentrate on preaching, free from the distractions of pastoral work, a privilege he soon turned down, recognizing that he could not preach if he did not know his hearers. In a statement that surprised many, he wrote in his autobiography, "I am commonly thought of as a preacher, but I should not put preaching central in my ministry. Personal counseling has been central."[4] Personal work with people in the congregation is vital to the preacher's life and ministry, including especially preaching.

The Preacher and God's Word

Most works on preaching deal with the preacher's responsibility to practice good exegesis of biblical texts in preparation for preaching, so I will not go into that issue here. My concern is to urge the preacher to let the Bible deal directly with him or her on a regular basis. By this I mean that we should read the Bible not only to determine its significance in its historical setting and not only to discover its message for the others in the congregation, but we should also read it as God's word to us. If we preachers do not hear God's word personally, we are taking seriously neither the power of that word nor our place within the congregation of God's people.

---

[3]For an extensive treatment of this see John S. McClure, *The Round-Table Pulpit: Where Leadership and Preaching Meet* (Nashville: Abingdon Press, 1995).

[4]Cited in Robert M. Miller, *Harry Emerson Fosdick: Preacher, Pastor, Prophet* (New York: Oxford University Press, 1985), 251.

However, the preacher, as a professional Bible reader and scholar, often finds it difficult to hear a text uncritically. We have learned to analyze texts, to identify their syntax, to look up the meanings of words. We have learned, in other words, to be in control of the text in order to discover its meaning. What can we do about this? How can we yield control to the text? One possibility that comes right out of our consideration of the oral background of scripture is to read texts aloud. After all, as we have seen, the texts were written with the expectation that they would be *heard*. Most people find it much easier to deal with a text objectively when reading it silently, but we discover that it is hard to keep the subjective self at bay when the words are pronounced and heard. Oral reading in the study is also good preparation for the reading of scripture in the service of worship. Most important, however, is our hearing the text as God's word to us personally.

There are audio- and videotapes of Bible reading available, and we can sometimes be helped by listening to others read a text on tape. Reading aloud to others is also helpful. We can do that by the bedside of a sick person or for children (ours or others'). As we read aloud, we are more likely to stop and experiment with different ways of emphasizing words and phrases, with various tones of voice, and with different systems of phrasing. Such experiments with hearing can lead us to surprising insights. Our Bible texts, most of which were dictated and meant to be read aloud, are full of possible tongue-in-cheek statements, ironic retorts, contemplative thoughts, bombastic pronouncements, and many other types of communication. None of these will be obvious on the written page until we attempt to turn them back into oral communication. We are much more likely to hear God's word for us personally when we hear it pronounced, even by our own voices.

The Preacher's Self-Expression

No matter how hard we try, we cannot hide our personalities when we are communicating. We might attempt to blend in with our profession by wearing clerical garb. We might wear the everyday suit of the business person in the congregation. We might train ourselves to speak in the generic tones of the television news anchorperson. We might also dress and speak down to try to blend with the more casual people around us. Nothing can disguise who we are when we open our mouths to speak. Whatever else we express, we express ourselves.

Ordinary people sense our self-expression. They easily detect a note of insincerity. They can tell from our preaching when we are angry or discouraged. They recognize also when we are sincere, when what we are saying is important to us, and (perhaps most important) when we care deeply for them. Thus, there is no escaping the involvement of our personalities in preaching, but as Phillips Brooks recognized, this is not just a problem to be dealt with, it is the heart of what it means to be God's spokesperson.[5]

It stands to reason then that it is important for the preacher to have a clear understanding of just what kind of person he or she is. A good seminary program includes the kind of self-assessment that can help a student toward that understanding. However, graduation from seminary is not the end of the process of self-understanding. We continue to surprise and sometimes shock ourselves with our reactions to certain people and to certain objects or events. If we are aware, we can continue the process of learning about ourselves throughout our lifetimes.

Such growth in understanding should make us not only better people but also better communicators. This is so partly because self-insight will help us to understand better why people respond to our preaching as they do. In his *Presence in the Pulpit*,[6] Hans van der Geest describes how preachers make various impressions on various hearers, some of those impressions having little to do with the actual person of the preacher and more to do with earlier experiences of the hearer. Such miscommunications the preacher cannot completely control, but knowing oneself can help the preacher to understand such dynamics and to deal with them.

Since preaching is, to a great extent, self-expression, it is foolish to pretend that the personal faith or morals of the preacher are unimportant. The integrity of the preacher has a direct bearing on the credibility of the sermon. Every generation in the history of the church has observed the ruin of ministries by the moral failings of preachers. We need to be circumspect when dealing with personal relationships and finances, where even the appearance of evil can be devastating. The trustworthiness and winsomeness of the preacher have a decisive impact on the attraction of the Lord on whose behalf the preacher preaches.

---

[5] See Phillips Brooks's classic Lyman Beecher Lectures of 1877, *Lectures on Preaching* (New York: E. P. Dutton, 1877), where he begins by naming the two elements in preaching as truth and personality.

[6] Hans van der Geest, *Presence in the Pulpit* (Atlanta: John Knox Press, 1981), 14–20.

For this reason, the preparation of the preacher to preach is at least as important as the preparation of the sermon to be preached. The preacher as a credible communicator, as a compassionate member of the congregation, and as an honorable part of the history of God's messengers will be an effective fellow worker with God, whose role in preaching we shall look at next.

10

Romans 10:17—Preaching as Means of Grace

I have never talked at any length with a preacher about preaching without the conversation turning to the topic of a mystery. Most seminary-educated preachers are analytical enough to want to explain everything they experience in a way understandable to most people. Therefore, when we encounter something we cannot understand through investigation, we make it a topic of conversation, especially when talking with others with similar experiences. It seems that we all have stories of people hearing things in our sermons that we are sure we never said and of people being strangely affected by sermons that we would evaluate as weaker than most. Perhaps the greater mystery is that we are at all surprised by such occurrences. It seems that we preach about the importance of people's depending on God for the outcome of any effort, but we fail to expect God to work in and through our preaching.

The reformers who put together the Second Helvetic Confession testified very early in that document (immediately after the section on scripture as the word of God):

> The preaching of the Word of God is the Word of God. Wherefore when this Word of God is now preached in the church by preachers lawfully called, we believe that the

129

very Word of God is proclaimed, and received by the faithful; and that neither any other Word of God is to be invented nor is to be expected from heaven: and that now the Word itself which is preached is to be regarded, not the minister that preaches; for even if he be evil and a sinner, nevertheless the Word of God remains still true and good.[1]

It appears that only under the influence of the Enlightenment did awareness of the direct activity of God in and through preaching fade from the preacher's experience. Preachers, influenced by modern scientific education, failed to develop a vocabulary that would allow them to speak of the role of the divine in a seemingly human task. It is, therefore, important for us at this point in our thinking about preaching and especially in light of the setting of the sun on the Enlightenment to consider the operation of divine presence in our preaching.

In chapter 1 we looked briefly at Romans 10 as we discussed a theology of the word for contemporary preaching. We considered it again in chapter 5 as we looked into Paul's epistles for pointers to oral communication, and in chapter 7, as we developed a philosophy of language for preaching the gospel. It is time now to return to that passage and attempt a clearer understanding of verse 17 in its context.

The larger context is Paul's concern (Romans 9—11) about the place of Israel in the ongoing plan of God for the salvation of the human race. This was probably more than a personal concern for Paul. In his book, *The Mystery of Romans: The Jewish Context of Paul's Letter*, Mark Nanos argues that Paul wrote the letter to call the Gentile Christians in Rome back to the Jewish roots of their faith.[2] His argument brings into question the tendency to interpret Romans as though it were linked to Galatians and thus to assume that Romans shares the invective of Galatians against the Judaisers. Discussion of this issue is not within the scope of this book, but to understand Paul's statements about the communication of the

---

[1]Cited here from the *Book of Confessions* (New York: General Assembly of the United Presbyterian Church in the U.S.A., 1970), par. 5.004.

[2]"Romans was not written to discourage association with Judaism, or even to challenge any 'judaising' tendencies, but quite the opposite. Romans was written to 'remind' the early church in Rome (composed almost entirely of Christian gentiles who were associating with Jews under the authority of the synagogue) of the importance of their 'obedience of faith.'" Mark D. Nanos, *The Mystery of Romans: The Jewish Context of Paul's Letter* (Minneapolis: Fortress Press, 1996), 34.

gospel in Romans 10, we must recognize the high respect for the Hebrew Bible and the Jewish people that he displays here.

Paul's quandary, of course, is his conviction that the Jewish people as a whole have rejected their Messiah, which brings the whole issue of God's plan of salvation into question. In Romans 9, Paul establishes the sovereignty of God over everything, including the process of salvation. Romans 10 opens with Paul's heart cry of hope that his kinfolk may be saved. The problem, he declares, is that they try to establish their own righteousness instead of submitting to God's righteousness made available in Jesus, the Messiah. Verse 4 then states: "For Christ is the end of the law so that there may be righteousness for everyone who believes."[3] The rest of chapter 10 deals with the implications of this righteousness by means of faith instead of by means of human effort.

Verses 5–8 present a *pesher*-type exposition and application of Deuteronomy 30:12–14. *Pesher* is the practice of the Essenes and others of applying texts of their Bible as prophetic of their own experience.[4] This Deuteronomy text appears in the heart of the final exhortation of Moses to his followers before relinquishing leadership to Joshua. As with final words in other situations, these were revered and accorded great authority by succeeding generations of Israelites and Jews. So Paul is referring to a word that carries its own authority among his kinfolk. He connects that word with his discussion of righteousness by faith by introducing it with a Leviticus text—18:5, "You shall keep my statutes and my ordinances; by doing so one shall live: I am the LORD." Paul quotes the Hebrew Bible as translated into Greek (LXX), so in Romans 10:5 we find, "the person who does these things will live by them." He has already established that nobody does these things completely, so nobody can live by them (Romans 1 and 2). Now he can introduce another quotation from Moses as an illustration of what it means to become righteous by faith.

---

[3]During the last decade controversy has again raged over the translation and significance of this verse—controversy accompanying the renewed interest in the relationship of Christianity and Judaism. Two recent versions are good examples of the controversy. *New Living Translation* (Wheaton: Tyndale House, 1996) has it: "For Christ has accomplished the whole purpose of the law. All who believe in him are made right with God." The *Contemporary English Version* (New York: American Bible Society, 1995) states: "But Christ makes the Law no longer necessary for those who become acceptable to God by faith." Both also have footnotes pointing to other options. Since this issue lies outside the purpose of our present discussion, we shall not pursue it further.

[4]For a helpful introduction to *pesher* see Richard Longenecker, *Biblical Exegesis in the Apostolic Period* (Grand Rapids, Mich.: Eerdmans, 1975), 38–45.

So here at the heart of Paul's argument, in fact at the heart of Paul's doctrine of salvation, he speaks as Moses spoke his last words to his people. In the context of first-century Judaism, it is hard to imagine a more powerful argument than putting one's thoughts in the words and the form of the final message from the great prophet and emancipator Moses. In addition, Paul uses an interpretive form familiar among first-century Jews: *pesher*. *Pesher*, as we noted above, was used extensively by the Qumran community, as well as others, to connect ancient passages to contemporary situations or persons. Acts 2:16 shows Peter using the same technique, when he says, "No, this is what was spoken through the prophet Joel." In our Romans passage, Paul inserts his comments into the quoted text, using three parenthetical statements that begin, "that is…" (*tout' estin*, vv. 6, 7, and 8).

The first of these statements of Moses is, "Do not say in your heart, 'who will ascend into heaven?'" Paul's *pesher* is, "that is, to bring Christ down." Christ, of course, has already come down and returned, so to try to bring him down again is both unnecessary and a sign of unbelief. The second Mosaic quotation is, "or 'Who will descend into the abyss?'" Paul's comment is, "that is, to bring Christ up from the dead." It is a given for Paul that Christ has already been brought up from the dead by God, so any attempt by humans to do so is ludicrous. The third sentence from Deuteronomy is a positive one, "The word [*rhema*] is near you, on your lips and in your heart." This statement propels Paul into his discussion of confession of faith and preaching, as he begins, "that is, the word of faith which we proclaim" (*to rhema tes pisteos ho kerussomen*).

In verses 9–13 Paul establishes that it is the confession "Jesus is Lord" that, when believed in the heart and confessed with the lips, saves people. This means justification for the individual believer and recognition that the former distinction between Jew and Gentile is now abolished. He finishes this part of his argument with a quotation from the prophet Joel (2:32 in our versions of Joel, 3:5 in the LXX): "Everyone who calls on the name of the LORD shall be saved." In early Israel, calling on the name of the Lord was a way of talking about prayer or worship of the Lord in general. So this quotation points more to a lifestyle than to a cry for help in a specific situation.

Paul then poses a series of rhetorical questions in verses 14 and 15: "But how are they to call on one in whom they have not believed? And how are they to believe in one of whom they have never heard? And how are they to hear without someone to proclaim him? And how are they to proclaim him unless they are sent?" He begins his response to this challenge by quoting part of Isaiah 52:7, "How beautiful are the feet of those who bring good news!" For Paul this establishes the fact that some have been sent and have gone. He will even more firmly establish that in verse 18 by quoting from Psalm 19 (18 in the LXX), "Their voice has gone out to all the earth, and their words to the ends of the world." In fact, the apostolic band and many others had by this time gone in many directions with the message of the Messiah.

Since we have discussed at some length (in chapters 2 through 5) the communication register of the first-century church in the matrix of Judaism, and since we are aware of the aura of authority in which the Jews and early Christians saw the Hebrew Bible, it should be clear that quoting on one subject from all three major sections of that Bible (Pentateuch, Prophets, and Writings) would be to speak or to write with overwhelming authority to Jews or Christians who had been heavily influenced by Jewish believers. Adding to that the observation that the Pentateuch quotation is composed of the last words of Moses to the people, we begin to see the extremely effective rhetoric of this Romans passage.

But Paul leaves us in verse 16 with his original quandary: "But not all have obeyed the good news" in spite of the fact that they have heard. Here he returns to Isaiah, this time to the familiar (especially to Christians) chapter 53. The quotation "Lord, who has believed our message?" is straight out of the LXX translation of the Hebrew, and it is vital for our understanding of verse 17 to trace the original wording here. The Greek reads *"kurie, tis episteusen te akoe hemon."* The next question in the Isaiah verse is "And to whom has the arm of the LORD been revealed?" If this is a doublet of Hebrew poetry, which seems to be the case, this second half indicates that the "message" referred to in the first half is divine revelation. We should keep in mind at this point that the testimony of the Hebrew Bible is that when a prophet speaks a word from the Lord (or a hearing/report), the Lord is active in the speaking and hearing. The claim of the prophets is that they deliver not a word *about* the Lord, but the word *of* the Lord. The connection that the apostle is making here with apostolic preaching is that in the apostolic reportage people are hearing the utterance of Christ himself.[5]

---

[5]Cf. Ernst Käsemann, *An die Römer* (Tübingen: J. C. B. Mohr, 1974), 285.

What word lies behind the term *message* or *akoe* in the Hebrew text? As we saw in chapter 5, it is a compound word, the root of which is the same as that of the word *shema*. This takes us back to the fundamental call to worship and confession of faith of all Israel—Deuteronomy 6:4, "Hear, O Israel: The LORD is our God, the LORD alone." That which is heard (*shema* = *akoe* = message) is also that which is passed on to others. Isaiah's good news, his report, which reveals the arm of the Lord who is the only God of Israel, brings us to Paul's statement in Romans 10:17: "So faith comes from what is heard, and what is heard comes through the word of Christ." The sentence structure links *pistis* (faith) as closely as possible with *akoe* (hearing or message) and also links *akoe* closely with *dia rhematos Christou* (through or by means of Christ's word). Tracing the significance of linking hearing, faith, and the word of Christ should bring us very close to the center of Paul's understanding of both salvation and preaching.

Paul has made it quite clear in Romans up to this point that since all have sinned, every person who is justified experiences a miracle of grace. And here in 10:17 he points to the agency of the miracle, the means of grace: the utterance of Christ, which is equivalent to the powerful (see 1:16), creative utterance of God and which is heard each time the preaching of the gospel awakens faith in an individual. The hearing that Paul is referring to here is not just paying attention to a conversation. It is, rather, a *shema* hearing, that is, responding to a summons—to a call for an encounter with God. It is the kind of hearing that recognizes the voice of the Lord and responds in "the obedience of faith" (1:5 and 16:26), calling on the name of the Lord.

This understanding is not universally accepted by scholars. However, I can muster three major names to support my understanding. Cranfield concludes his all too brief look at verse 17 with these words, "Faith results from hearing the message, and the hearing of the message comes about through the word of Christ (i.e., through Christ's speaking the message by the mouths of His messengers)."[6] Ulrich Wilkens puts it, "In the word of faith Christ himself speaks and acts, as God himself acts in the word of the prophets."[7]

---

[6]C. E. B. Cranfield, *The Epistle to the Romans,* International Critical Commentary (Edinburgh: T. & T. Clark, 1975), 537.

[7]This is my translation of his "Im Wort des Glaubens spricht und handelt Christus selbst, wie im Wort der Propheten Gott selbst handelt." Ulrich Wilkens, *Der Brief an die Römer,* Evangelisch-Katholischer Kommentar zum Neuen Testament, vol. 2 (Zürich: Benziger/Neukirchener Verlag, 1980), 229.

We find an even stronger statement in Schlier. Speaking of the phrase "through the word of Christ," he concludes,

> It is...the source of *akoe* along with that of *pistis*; but not as "the assignment and commission of Jesus" (Lietzmann, Michel)—*rhema* cannot mean that—also not as "the preaching of Christ" (Maier, Käsemann), but as the "act-word" of Christ, which has revealed itself to the apostle according to Galatians 1:12 and 16 through the *apokalupsis Iesou.*[8]

This discussion is not just an exercise in interpretation. As mentioned at the outset of this chapter, every preacher has had experiences of the effect of preaching that cannot be explained by an analysis of human communication. We have all had to admit from time to time that a sermon has exerted a more profound influence than we can take credit for. In fact, it is all too often the sermons that we would evaluate as weak that move people in strange ways. This is no excuse for the preparation of weak sermons. If God is to employ our words as the very words of Christ, then we should make sure that our words are of the highest quality and clarity possible for us. Such a realization should, on the other hand, teach the preacher the humility of the apostle Paul, who wrote about preaching:

> For since, in the wisdom of God, the world did not know God through wisdom, God decided, through the foolishness of our proclamation, to save those who believe. For Jews demand signs and Greeks desire wisdom, but we proclaim Christ crucified, a stumbling block to Jews and foolishness to Gentiles, but to those who are the called, both Jews and Greeks, Christ the power of God and the wisdom of God. For God's foolishness is wiser than human wisdom, and God's weakness is stronger than human strength. (1 Cor. 1:21–25)

What does this imply for the process of preparing a sermon? In the appendices of this work, I include several sermons and comments on them to illustrate the thrust of my thinking. I offer here some observations on the preparation of those and similar sermons.

---

[8]Heinrich Schlier, *Der Römerbrief* (Freiburg: Herder, 1977), 318, (au. trans.).

First, I see no substitute for work on the biblical text of the sermon—work that is both extensive and intensive. I recognize the time constraints on most preachers, but I reiterate that there is nothing more important than consistent and deep reading of, and grappling with, the texts of the Bible. The New Common Lectionary offers us texts in a *lectio continua* fashion, so that we can preach through books of the Bible. Thus, we need not do the background reading and preliminary thinking every week. Once we begin preaching on a book, we can concentrate on individual texts from week to week. I find it helpful to have a checklist of questions or issues to apply to each text.[9] Such a practice can help us avoid overlooking any exegetical approach that might prove helpful.

In addition to good exegetical work, the preacher should also think theologically about the text, asking what the text at hand says or implies about God and related theological issues. This will often lead naturally to the "So what?" questions that are vital to our preaching. Here the primary question is, What does this text want to do with its hearers? I have found it helpful to have a group of people from the congregation meet with me regularly to ask such questions and tell me what they see in the text for their needs.

At this point, the preparation process should change from one in which the preacher is in control to one in which the text takes over and confronts the preacher personally. Such a "turning of the tables" becomes the transition from an academic study of a text to preparing to preach. Getting from here to the sermon is rarely easy, but it is a rather simple journey. It includes deciding what the text wants to accomplish in the lives of those who hear the sermon. This is what I call a statement of the aim of the sermon. Then we can decide what we need to say to the audience to accomplish that aim. This is the sermon idea. Just how to say it sometimes comes easily, and at other times only with a struggle. If we understand where our hearers will be in relation to the text as we begin, we should be able to develop a beginning for the sermon. If we have a clear picture of our aim, we should be able to develop an end. The rest of the sermon is a matter of getting there from here, using language appropriate to our hearers.

---

[9]A good one is available in Ronald J. Allen, *Contemporary Biblical Interpretation for Preaching* (Valley Forge, Pa.: Judson Press, 1984), 139–43.

It will be obvious to anybody who has tried to preach that the foregoing is a nearly criminal oversimplification, for which I apologize. My only justification is that I do not intend this book to be a how-to book on preaching. There are many good homiletics books available that guide the reader step-by-step through the process of sermon preparation and preaching. My assumption here is that the reader is already following the good advice of instructors and writers and can apply to that knowledge and experience the insights of orality studies for our new millennium.

Our study in the early chapters of this book has shown us the human side of communication in the early church. Now we have had a glimpse of the divine mystery of preaching and what that might mean for our preparation. The communication to others of what we have heard from Christ is more than oratory. It is revelation. If we give God room to work in our enterprise, people will hear and respond to God's word. God can, of course, work in spite of us, but we can hardly doubt that we should work with God to fulfill our calling and commission. Therefore, as we noted in chapter 9, our preparation to preach should be bathed in prayer, and our sermons should be offered to God as an act of worship— an act that involves both preacher and hearers. Such preparation involves stringent personal discipline, thorough work on text and sermon, and the involvement of one's whole being in the speaking. Christian preaching demands much from the preacher, but it also offers the opportunity to be a fellow worker with God and the experience of witnessing others hearing and responding to the voice of Christ.

11

Orality, Hermeneutics, and Homiletics

Language is interpretive. Every instance of linguistic communication is an attempt to interpret what is actual, that is, objects, events, experiences, feelings, and so forth, so that the recipient of the communication can, in a sense, stand near the object or in the event, experience, or feeling—can *understand* the actual. Thus, every speech act or written document is hermeneutical. It interprets the actual by means of linguistic symbols.

In chapter 10 we saw how Paul's use of language in Romans 10 interpreted the common experience of the surprising impact of the human word in preaching. Paul's theological interpretation of that phenomenon included its roots in God's revelation through Moses and its continuing reality in Christian preaching that results in faith.

Preaching, as one specific language act, is certainly interpretive. Preaching has as its objective the interpretation of the actuality of the divine in mundane human existence, which is quite similar to what we saw Paul doing in Romans 10. If that is not what a preacher is trying to accomplish, she or he might better call the communicating something other than Christian preaching. If, as I would hope, the preacher intends to offer the hearers a language by which they can actualize God and the whole divine realm in which they, as Christians, live, then that preacher must realize that preaching is basically interpretation. If that is true, then homiletics is hermeneutics. Not every interpretive act is preaching, of course, but every valid sermon is interpretation of life as faith perceives it.

Given this close relationship between interpretation and preaching, it is important for us to consider the role of the human voice in the interpretation of scripture. For too long homileticians have confined themselves to the process of sermon preparation and presentation, while biblical hermeneutics has become a primarily literary endeavor. Robin Meyers' statement to this point is worth quoting in full:

> Perhaps the single biggest failure in the teaching of preaching is that young ministers are not fully impressed with the difference between textuality and orality. Shaped by mountains of books, called upon to write scores of papers, and graded largely by what they commit to the page, aspiring preachers train the eye but neglect the ear. Yet it is to the world of sound that they will go, plying their wares acoustically. The major moments of public ministry (the sermon, the funeral eulogy, the marriage ceremony) are all rhetorical moments. No one will see their outlines, much less grade them. Rather, as Jesus warned, "By their *words* they will be justified, by their *words* they will be condemned."[1]

I suggest that it is high time for the homiletical guild once again (before Schleiermacher our neat categories hardly existed!) to offer our understanding of the dynamics of oral communication to the guild of Bible scholars. Some of those scholars are fascinated with the recent research in rhetoric, in oral tradition, or in orality studies, which offers them an alternative to the exclusively literary approaches of the last two centuries.

One reason for this fascination is the frustration over the failure of *Formgeschichte* to accomplish what it set out to do. The desire of the form critics was to get behind the literature of the Bible to the oral forms used by Israel and the early church and to view those

---

[1]Robin R. Meyers, *With Ears to Hear: Preaching as Self-Persuasion* (Cleveland: Pilgrim Press, 1993), 21.

forms in their original *Sitze im Leben* (life settings). For whatever reasons, the scholars involved in this enterprise in the late nineteenth and early twentieth centuries identified many forms but did not, as far as I can see, really get a glimpse of the use of those forms in their primarily oral cultures. I suspect that the problem derived from the difficulty of escaping from the confines of literary thinking, which formed the primary paradigm of Western culture at the time.

The careful research done by orality scholars in the last fifty years and the loosening up of our general understanding of communication stimulated by the technologies of radio and television have laid the groundwork for an important new avenue of the study of biblical documents. As we have seen, the documents themselves make it obvious that they were not produced by individuals sitting quietly with stylus or quill in hand carefully formulating thoughts on parchment, papyrus, or wax. Rather, for the most part, they were probably spoken by one person and written down by a professional scribe. Careful research indicates that no more than 10 percent of the population of the Roman Empire even as late as the time of Christ was actually literate.[2] This was probably true even among Palestinian Jews, many of whom learned to sound out the Hebrew Scriptures, but few of whom ever attempted to write anything. Apparently even most people who could write chose instead to employ an amanuensis to do the job for them. Tertius even identifies himself in Romans 16:22 as the writer of Paul's letter to Rome. And Paul, in Galatians 6:11, points to his own handwriting, which must have been obviously different from that of the scribe who wrote down the rest of the letter.

Scholars have also come to understand that a letter like Romans, addressed as it is to a whole community of people, would as a matter of course be read aloud at one or more assemblies of the intended recipients, along with appropriate commentary and explanation by the carrier of the document, who in this case was Phoebe. Both the relative scarcity of people with good reading skills and the difficulties of copying made this method the most practical way to communicate to large groups.

---

[2]William V. Harris, *Ancient Literacy* (Cambridge, Mass.: Harvard University Press, 1989), 21–22.

In other words, the documents were spoken into being, with a scribe transforming them into written form to be carried over distances and time; then they were spoken back into life by one or more people who read them to their intended recipients. For this reason, Rudolf Bohren wrote, "The texts should become again what they were originally: spoken word, preached sermon."[3] If Bohren (and Ebeling, Bonhoeffer, and others) is right, transforming a written text of the Bible is far from tampering with the text—it is rather bringing the text to its intended end. Preachers then should have no hesitation in bringing our understanding of oral communication into the process of coming to an understanding of the text.

What effect would an approach from the standpoint of orality studies have on an understanding of the text? We should admit at the outset that there are some texts in the Bible, such as the books of Kings and Chronicles, that are primarily literary. A study of oral backgrounds would most likely contribute little to the interpretation of such texts. But the vast majority of biblical texts can be brought to life in helpful ways by recognizing them as basically written records of oral communication.

In some instances we are led by the text itself to read as though we were hearing. This is obviously the case when we read the declamations of the prophets, the teaching episodes of Jesus, or the preaching of the book of Acts. It is less obvious and far too often overlooked in the case of narratives and epistles. Gilbert Bartholomew has helped us toward this understanding in his article "Feed My Lambs: John 21:15–19 as Oral Gospel."[4] David Barr has offered similar insight in his article "The Apocalypse of John as Oral Enactment."[5] In a chapter of her book *The Cloister Walk*, Kathleen Norris tells of staying in a Benedictine monastery and hearing the book of Revelation read aloud during the Easter season. Her comments on that experience are interesting, especially this passage:

---

[3]Bohren, *Predigtlehre*, 148. The above is my own translation of Bohren's "Die texte sollen wieder werden, was sie waren, gesprochenes Wort, gepredigte Predigt."

[4]Gilbert L. Bartholomew, "Feed My Lambs: John 21:15–19 as Oral Gospel," in *Semeia* 39 (1987): 69–96.

[5]David L. Barr, "The Apocalypse of John as Oral Enactment," *Interpretation* 40, no. 3 (July 1986): 243–56.

Ironically, it was hearing Revelation read aloud that allowed me to re-examine the way I'd always stereotyped the book as "hell-fire and damnation." Engaging the book as a listener forced me to consider the awesome power of metaphor, and how thoroughly it defeats our attempts to contain it. We do not value it for what it is, a unique form of truth-telling, and that is precisely what John's Apocalypse seemed to be: uniquely true, true in its own terms, and indefinable—or just plain weird—outside them. Its images radically subvert our desire to literalize them, and also expose the flimsiness of our attempts to do so. Mainstream and liberal Christians may denounce apocalyptic imagery as negative thinking, and fundamentalists may try to defuse them by interpreting them as simple prediction. But the Book of Revelation comes with a built-in irony. Whether one believes that John wrote the book, or regards God as the true author of all scripture, to interpret its images so literally is to show a strange disregard for the method its author employs.[6]

These and other analyses indicate that important insights can be gained from the study of biblical documents as "oral texts." I place those two words in quotation marks both because they seem oxymoronic and because they are being used in this way as part of the technical jargon of orality studies. An oral text is approached as a record in the medium of writing of what was originally experienced as oral communication. Scholars for several decades have been reading the works of Homer, as well as documents such as *Beowulf*, *El Cid*, and *The Heliand*, assuming that they were recorded in writing by a scribe listening to a bard telling the story. Such a reading is enlivened by insights gained through the recording and studying of twentieth-century bards in Turkey, Ireland, and the former Yugoslavia.[7]

A list of peculiarities of oral communication in a primarily oral culture has been offered to us by Walter Ong:

---

[6]Kathleen Norris, *The Cloister Walk* (New York: Riverhead Books, 1996), 212.

[7]It pains me to consider what has happened recently to the cultures and individuals in Bosnia and Croatia who were trying to preserve the oral traditions of that area in oral forms. Much of it has been captured on audio recordings, but the living voices might prove to have been stilled forever.

1. Stereotyped or formulaic expression.
2. Standardization of themes.
3. Epithetic identification for "disambiguation" of classes or individuals.
4. Generation of "heavy" or ceremonial characters.
5. Formulary, ceremonial appropriation of history.
6. Cultivation of praise or vituperation.
7. Copiousness—repetition, parallelisms, synonyms, etc.[8]

In addition to these characteristics, which seem to be found in the communication of nearly all oral cultures, each culture developed some of its own marks of oral communication. Aristotle and others attempted to collect into handbooks of rhetoric and poetics the general approaches to persuasion and narration of their Hellenistic culture, as did Hillel and others for the Jewish culture. So we have at our disposal the information we need to begin to understand how public speech was formed and performed in ancient Israel and in the Roman Empire. We need now to go to the scriptures as examples of speech recorded by scribes.

An example that recently caught my attention is Romans 2: 1–11. Here the apostle turns from his rather vivid but analytical description of the basic sinfulness of Gentile peoples and begins to speak directly to what commentators refer to as an imaginary interlocutor.[9] I search in vain for a commentary that attempts to picture Paul dictating the letter to Tertius and slipping very naturally into a mode of prophetic preaching at this point, as he deals with the sinfulness of the human race. If we can visualize that picture, we can begin to appreciate the poetic repetition and rhythm, the rhetorical reiteration, the mnemonic chiasm, the vivid description, and the fine balance of generalities and particularities that must have marked Paul's preaching. Let us seek out in this passage Ong's marks of oral communication, as well as other signs of the spoken word.

Most scholars now recognize that much of what Paul has said in chapter 1 echoes statements in Wisdom of Solomon 12—15 and other texts of diaspora Judaism, which offer him some standard themes (2). He appears also to have used several standard

---

[8]Ong, *Interfaces of the Word.*
[9]Cf. James D. G. Dunn, *Romans 1—8,* Word Biblical Commentary 38A (Dallas: Word Books, 1988), 89f.

formulaic (1) expressions in that description, which would serve a double purpose. It would both bring to the attention of the Gentile believers the gravity of sin among the Gentiles and strike a familiar note of concern among the Jewish believers about the Gentiles. At that point Paul turns to the sin of judgment, which creates a bridge to the sin of the Jews.

Romans 2:1–4

Therefore you have no excuse, whoever you are, when you judge others; for in passing judgment on another you condemn yourself, because you, the judge, are doing the very same things. You say, "We know that God's judgment on those who do such things is in accordance with truth." Do you imagine, whoever you are, that when you judge those who do such things and yet do them yourself, you will escape the judgment of God? Or do you despise the riches of his kindness and forbearance and patience? Do you not realize that God's kindness is meant to lead you to repentance?

In chapter 2, as he turns his attention to the sinfulness of the Jews, he begins with the sin of judging others. He gives us a good example of copiousness (7) by using the word *judge* four times in verse 1, in a marvelously well-balanced statement. His abrupt shift from the third person plural analytical form to the second person singular direct and confrontational form is followed by his designating the hearer as the one judging (*pas ho krinon*). He then uses a brief chiasm to tell them that in judging others they judge, or condemn, themselves (*krineis ton, seauton katakrineis*). Thus, the judger has no more excuse than does the Gentile sinner (compare 2:1 and 1:20).

The NRSV translators think that Paul's beginning the next sentence with "we know" (*oidamen*) indicates that he means to use a common statement of his hearers against them. This is certainly possible; furthermore, it is understandable as an application of the diatribe style of public speaking. If by their own admission they believe that God judges according to truth (*kata aletheian*), they have no reason to reckon on escaping divine judgment when they usurp God's prerogative and judge others.

The question in verse 4 makes an even harsher accusation, but does so in a way that would not destroy an antagonist. The negative word in the question is the verb, and Paul saves it until the end. "Or the riches of his kindness and forbearance and patience are you *despising*, knowing that God's kindness leads you to repentance?"[10] This soft approach is followed by the direct and harsh warning of verse 5: "By your hard and impenitent heart you are storing up wrath for yourself on the day of wrath when God's righteous judgment will be revealed." Here we see Paul refusing to do the typical disambiguation (3) and generation of heavy characters (4), since he wants not so much to win an argument as to lead people to God's grace.

Verse 6 is a succinct general statement, permitting some relaxation from what might be received as a withering accusation: "[God] will repay according to each one's deeds." This statement, which would likely have been accepted by all believers, is followed by an explanatory statement in chiastic form:

> To those who by patiently doing good seek for glory and honor and immortality, he will give eternal life; while for those who are self-seeking and who obey not the truth but wickedness, there will be wrath and fury. There will be anguish and distress for everyone who does evil, the Jew first and also the Greek, but glory and honor and peace for everyone who does good, the Jew first and also the Greek. (Rom. 2:7–10)

As we see, Paul in this last member of the chiasm over-emphasizes the positive side by listing three instead of two results. This is quite common with Paul and seems to be a good technique of oral rhetoric to ensure that the fine balance of the structure of thought does not remain so fine as to become soporific. At the same time, he makes his point very clear by both promising reward and warning about punishment.

Verse 11 is another general statement, which restates the intent of verse 6, but does so in a way that emphasizes the personhood and justice (righteousness) of God: "For God shows no partiality." In verses 12–16, Paul reverts to the third person plural analytical style, which he deserts in verse 17 once again to return to the second person singular style of prophetic preaching. For our purposes, however, it is enough to note the flow of thought through the very intense direct address of verses 1–11. Verse 1

---

[10]Author's translation.

warns the hearer against human judgment, and verse 2 follows with a warning of God's eschatological judgment. Verses 3 and 4 are designed to make the hearer conscious of her or his own culpability with reference to God's judgment. Verses 5 and 6 specify the situation of both the sinner and God so as to clarify the warning in verse 1. The chiasm in verses 7–10 forms a rhetorical expansion of verse six, describing in some detail the mode of divine judgment. Verse 11 completes the brief sermon by reiterating in a more personal way the picture of God offered in verse 6.

The theological depth of Romans has for centuries been lauded and learned from. It is high time that we begin to appreciate the preacher behind the theology. The logic of the whole epistle is the logic of the gospel: sin and salvation, with their many implications in time and eternity. And if we miss that proclamatory aspect, we miss the heart of both Romans and its author, not to mention the heart of God! If we try to *hear* the preacher producing the epistle as we study the text, then some of the passion in the original setting should begin to bleed through into our preaching. Our contemporary hearers are not, of course, first-century Roman believers, but that is no excuse for presenting cadavers instead of breathing organisms as sermons.

Paul's dramatic diatribe style, which he appears to have learned from both the Cynics and the Stoics, as well as from the rabbis, is still a useful way to preach. There may also be other ways to present dramatically the form and function of a text, but students of preaching as well as practicing preachers should be encouraged to sound out the biblical text so that they can hear it. Reading aloud draws one's attention to interpretive questions that scanning with the eye would not uncover. How would Isaiah have phrased and emphasized his, "Here am I; send me!" (Isa. 6:8)? How would Jesus have delivered his "eye of a needle" statement (Mk. 10:25 and parallels)? Matters of intonation, emphasis, and phrasing are most often neglected in literary commentaries. Oral interpretation can lead the preacher to levels of communication in or behind the text that would otherwise remain untouched.

We do not often stop to consider it, but day-to-day conversation is holistic communication. We convey not only thoughts but also emotions by the way we communicate. Such full communication does not depend on word, grammar, and syntax alone. It uses posture, facial expression, gesture, and vocal intonation simultaneously, sometimes adding objects or costumes as visual props. Not only the words of the speech but also the music and the dance participate in evoking meaning and feeling in the hearers. If the preacher is to accomplish such multilevel communication in the sermon, that preacher must recognize the same fullness in the biblical text and its context.

For the sake of both the preacher's understanding of the text and the preacher's ability to move people by means of the sermon, it is important for that preacher to pronounce aloud the text early in the process of preparing to preach. Such oral interpretation is not to take the place of a close reading of the text, with all the aids available. Since biblical texts are literature originally produced in ancient cultures and languages, any modern understanding and application of them deserves a careful reading through the methods of literary and historical study. However, to touch their origin we need to speak and to hear them; to prepare to preach them we need also to speak and to hear them.

12

Preaching Today and Tomorrow

The preacher is charged with a seemingly impossible task. Stepping into the role of preacher in the presence of a worshiping congregation, the preacher is expected to speak to those hearers a word from God. The hearer wants that word in understandable and applicable terms and forms. It must be both true to the tradition (now nearly two millennia old) and relevant to contemporary life. This challenge is enough to make any conscientious person resign in despair. How are we to proceed?

Review

In the first chapters of this book, we considered the general history of human communication, as well as Jesus and the early church in their communication situations. It is time now to think about how the forms of human communication are changing as we enter the twenty-first century and what that means for Christian preaching.

We noted earlier the radical change that occurred when the printed word became so common that whole societies began to think and even to speak in a literary fashion, avoiding redundancy and attempting to be original. We saw also that in a primarily oral culture such thinking would make little sense. Even where notes or a manuscript might be used in preparation or presentation, the sermon would be understood as the event that

149

happens between speaker and hearers in the moment of oral communication. The same notes might be used on several different occasions, but a preacher would never think that it was the same sermon. Reports that have come down to us show that the usual pattern was for a public speaker to speak on the basis of an organization developed mentally, with little aid of writing, and either to write out the speech from memory afterward or to edit the notes of a listener later to send somewhere or to keep for posterity.[1]

The situation was similar in the case of narratives. The preachers and teachers of the early church told the same stories and made the same applications over and over again, which was consistent with the practice in their cultures in general; but they would not have thought, as we do, that they were telling different versions of the same story. Even today, people living in primarily oral situations are confused by our questions about an original tale of which a later telling is but a version. The story is always the same yet always original in performance. The parables of Jesus and the reports of his miracles, the latter which I have called heroic tales about Jesus, would in the normal course of first-century communication have been told many times with differences of detail as called for by each specific audience or objective. The way the early Christian preachers and teachers told the stories was determined not by our modern concern for historical accuracy so much as by the occasion of their telling. The community of believers would ensure the general integrity of the narrative, while the teller would feel free to narrate in such a way as to make his or her desired impact on the hearers.

So we see a substantive difference between the communication register of the first century and that of the nineteenth century, from which many of our hermeneutical and homiletical models and methods come.

Even more to the point than the example of the first century is the difficulty that preachers are having at the threshold of the twenty-first century getting the Christian message through to

---

[1]Anthony J. Palmeri, "Ramism, Ong, and Modern Rhetoric," in *Media, Consciousness, and Culture*, ed. Bruce E. Gronbeck, Thomas J. Farrell, and Paul A. Soukup (Newbury Park, Calif.: Sage Publications, 1991), points out that "ancient orators typically wrote out a speech after its delivery." He continues, "Eighteenth-century elocutionists were concerned with oral delivery conceived of as reading from a text" (59). The similar pattern in nineteenth-century America is well illustrated by Garry Wills in *Lincoln at Gettysburg: The Words That Remade America* (New York: Touchstone, 1992).

people. Those who study such matters tell us that in the West, even though church attendance is staying rather constant, Christian morality is slipping seriously. Somehow the message of the cross, which became the point of orientation for early Christian living, is now seen as an interesting relic. Sermon listeners seem much more interested in personal security than in suffering for Christ. They are more concerned with self-esteem than with repentance. We preachers are trying many means of holding attention and of breaking through mental defenses, but we seem in most cases to be failing. We need to look seriously at the way we think about the sermon and the resultant preparation and preaching.

The Challenge

We can easily see why Walter Ong has characterized the new era as "secondary orality."[2] Both television and computers use an interesting mixture of aural and visual sensory experiences to convey not so much a message as a feeling. An executive of MTV recently pointed out that the means of communication used by that channel, watched faithfully by millions of teenagers is:

> not linear, like normal television; we're not dealing with plot and continuity, we're dealing with emotion, which is an entirely new way to use that television set. The only people who can understand the new way to use that television set are the people who grew up with it…They will accept almost everything over that screen.[3]

The domination of MTV and other television and film forms that follow its lead (including even the evening news telecasts) seems to be resulting in a generation of people who have great difficulty with the sequential and consequential thinking that their elders take for granted. My son, who recently was teaching logic in a major university, tells me that he sees an astounding lack of ability among young adults to recognize cause-and-effect sequences. The older "linear" communication is already coming into open conflict in schools and universities with the newer trend

---

[2]Ong, *The Presence of the Word*, 87–110, and *Orality and Literacy*, 136f.
[3]Quoted in "Ad Nauseam," 33; cited in Quentin Schultze and Roy Anker, *Dancing in the Dark: Youth, Popular Culture, and the Electronic Media* (Grand Rapids, Mich.: Eerdmans, 1991), 205.

toward communication of images and sound bites without connecting plots but with a frontal assault on moods.

Living through radical change is threatening and confusing to both the older, more traditional thinkers and to the younger people who are somehow involved in leading the change. In such a situation we should ask some basic questions about the communication challenges.

Is it important for preachers to make adjustments in the ways we communicate in light of all this? Haven't teenagers always developed their own peculiar means of communication? That may be true, but what we are seeing now is not so much teenagers developing a secret in-group vocabulary. We are seeing creative adults capitalizing on that tendency in young people and surrounding them and us with a whole new form of human consciousness. At the 1981 groundbreaking ceremony for a fourteen-million-dollar cinema-television school at the University of Southern California, George Lucas, a major creative genius of the modern film industry, said,

> For better or worse, the influence of the church, which used to be all-powerful, has been usurped by film. Films and television tell us the way we conduct our lives, what is right and wrong. It's important that the people who make films have ethics classes, philosophy classes, history classes. Otherwise we're witch-doctors.[4]

If that is true, and I see no need to argue with his assessment, then we preachers need to break out of our literate ways of thinking and prepare for effective communication in this borderland between the older culture of primary literacy and the coming culture of secondary orality.

What Shall We Do?

How can we effect such a change? First, we should recall that the development of new media of communication has never totally displaced the old media. People continued to speak after they learned to write; they continued to write by hand after the invention of the printing press and the typewriter; they continued to read after the introduction of the radio and the telephone; and people will continue to read, use the telephone, and listen to the

---

[4]Cited in Schultze and Anker, *Dancing in the Dark*, 110.

radio as the visual/speech image bites of television, computers, and whatever other technologies lie in the future become more pervasive. Therefore, we can be confident that our reading and writing are not becoming irrelevant. We need, however, to understand them as tools to get the communication job done and not as ends in themselves.

We are being presented with some new tools. Many of us are already at home with computers. I am writing this book on one. We also watch a lot of television. What we must do is try to understand how these media are affecting the way people receive and process information. Starting with Marshall McLuhan, there have been several helpful analyses of the effects of communication media on the thought patterns of their users.[5] Almost any of these can help us to see the major developments relative to the communication situation facing us. All of them bring us to the realization that we must understand our hearers better if we are going to communicate effectively. Only when we get a grasp of the way people receive and process information can we hope to present the gospel as information that they can assimilate.

Since the total context of a given communication situation is becoming even more important than in the past (the cinematographers call it "ground"), we preachers must focus on the assembled congregation as the primary context for preaching. We should probe to discover how our congregations understand themselves when they gather on Sunday morning—and how they understand the preacher. What is their perceived purpose in gathering, and how does the preacher help them to fulfill that purpose?

As part of our regular sermon preparation process, we should do at least a quick mental demographic survey of our hearers. The better we know the people, the less time this will take, but it is important not to assume that we know enough about them. Congregations, especially in North America, are always changing. People die, move away, grow, become incapacitated. New life situations develop every week—marital stress, divorce, coping with aging parents, births, deaths, and changes at school, work,

---

[5]In addition to the commonly cited books of McLuhan and the works of Walter Ong to which I referred above, I recommend Pierre Babin, *The New Era in Religious Communication*, trans. David Smith (Minneapolis: Fortress Press, 1991); Quentin Schultze, ed., *American Evangelicals and the Mass Media* (Grand Rapids, Mich.: Academie Books, 1990), Schultze and Anker, *Dancing in the Dark*; and Leonard I. Sweet, ed., *Communication and Change in American Religious History* (Grand Rapids, Mich.: Eerdmans, 1993).

and in the community. Given such changes, even if the same people are present week after week (which is highly unusual), their interests and needs are ever changing. On the pastoral level, we remain at least partially aware of this, but we too rarely take it into account as we prepare to preach. Sermon preparation should include prayers for the people who will hear the sermon.

In addition to that focus on the congregation, we need to use our imaginations to develop more appropriate ways of preparing to preach in the communication situations of today and tomorrow. One way we can do this is to focus on the use of words and phrases to elicit images and remembered emotions in our hearers. This aspect of preaching has always been important, but now it must be considered primary. One means to this end is the use of stories. In East Tennessee (where I now live), storytelling has never died, but it has made an astounding resurgence in the last five years because of the National Storytelling Festival in Jonesborough, Tennessee, each fall. Ten thousand or more people travel to that little town every October to tell and hear stories of all sorts, including Bible stories. Similar festivals are springing up all over the United States and also in other countries. The use of stories in preaching and teaching is certainly not new. Indeed, Jesus is considered one of history's master story crafters and tellers. At one point Mark's gospel states, "he did not speak to them except in parables, but he explained everything in private to his disciples" (Mk. 4:34). Both testaments of our Bible are examples of the narrator's art. Much of the early Christian preaching recorded in Acts includes the retelling of the story of God's relationship with the people of Israel. A well-told story touches a part of the human psyche that no syllogism can reach. For this reason, toward the end of the twentieth century, the story form developed from a technique of illustrating abstract ideas in sermons to the very form of sermons themselves in the style called narrative preaching.[6] Such preaching includes not just sermons that tell stories but also such presentations as dramatic monologues or even dramatic conversation sermons. In my sermon "Radical Trust" (see appendix 1), I attempt to engage the imaginations of my hearers

[6]See James Sanders, *God Has a Story Too: Sermons in Context* (Philadelphia: Fortress Press, 1979); Edmund Steimle, Morris Niedenthal, and Charles Rice, *Preaching the Story* (Philadelphia: Fortress Press, 1980); Wayne Robinson, ed., *Journeys toward Narrative Preaching* (New York: Pilgrim Press, 1990); and Eugene L. Lowry, *The Homiletical Plot* (Atlanta: John Knox Press, 1980).

with the implications of the incarnation of Jesus for the Christian life. I make this leap by means of the story of Jesus' sending of disciples to proclaim the reign of God. A simple shift of body position helps to carry the dramatized stories in this presentation.

However, narrative preaching cannot do everything that needs to be done. We need also to recognize the interactivity that is coming on strongly from many sides. Hypermedia in our computers and increasing responsiveness from our televisions will make it harder and harder for people to sit quietly and listen to sermons. We must try to bring more than the auditory sense into direct play in the preaching moment. The pervasiveness of the television screen makes it important for us to offer more movement than is customary in church. Where is it written that the preacher must never move from behind the pulpit or even that the preacher must always face the audience? What is the advantage of the preacher's being "up there" while the rest of us are "down here"? We preachers might not feel comfortable as television talk-show hosts on Sunday morning, but more activity and interactivity will become increasingly important.[7]

In "Radical Trust," mentioned above, I move from one side of the pulpit to the other and eventually to the aisle among the hearers, where I stand facing the pulpit as I voice questions of the contemporary congregation. I tried it in Japan in the chapel of Tokyo Union Seminary. There the response was mixed. After complimenting me on the sermon, several students and faculty members said that they doubted a Japanese preacher could do such a presentation. There are places and congregations where traditional ways of doing things in church have so strong a hold that experimentation is next to impossible. Knowing that, I still think it is worth the risk to try new ways of communicating in an ever-changing culture of communication.

It is also helpful in some situations to be more direct than usual with our hearers. Appendix 2 is a sermon called "Performing the Gospel." In it I attempt to do more than just talk about the gospel. I try with both verbal and bodily language to enact the gospel of forgiveness in such a way as to touch the deep need of forgiveness in the human heart. Speaking a simple sentence ("Friend, your sins are forgiven you") directly to people, even calling individuals by name, causes a deep interaction between preacher and people

---

[7]See Stephenson Bond, *Interactive Preaching* (St. Louis: CBP Press, 1991).

and, we would hope, between people and God. In the case of this sermon, the repetition of the sentence of forgiveness that Jesus said to the paralytic has led some hearers to tears of joy and great relief.

Thinking about multisensory communication should stimulate us to think more deeply about the immediate context of most of our preaching, that is, the service of worship. In the experience of corporate worship, we have the opportunity to lead every sense of every worshiper into action. The interactivity of the singing, the praying, the unison and responsive readings, and the climactic interactivity and multisensory experience of the Lord's supper can, on one hand, cause the preaching to seem tame in contrast or, on the other hand, can set the scene for active participation in the performance of the gospel.

Some Suggestions

How can preaching cope with such change as we are now facing in our age of television and computers? That is our challenge. The whole picture is still incomplete, but I can make several suggestions that I think will be important.

1. We need to implement more interaction with our congregations. This will be easier with young people than with our senior citizens. Older folks have been conditioned to sit silently to hear a sermon. The primary exception to this is the African American congregation, where oral and visual response to preaching is not only tolerated but expected. On the other hand, computers are encouraging people to control the rate at which they learn, so it appears that as a computer-literate generation matures, it will become increasingly important to give hearers a voice in how preachers present a message. In my sermon "Not Only Human" (appendix 3), I begin by asking for input from the congregation, and I have been pleasantly surprised by the open response even in rather conservative congregations.

2. We need to move around more as we preach. People on television dramas and game shows are either moving or the cameras are moving around them. Even the news includes graphics and on-site video. Thus, the so-called talking head is becoming boring. I preached the sermon "Radical Trust" in a college chapel setting, where some

students were videotaping the service. One of them later mentioned to me that my changing positions was like the changing of camera angles so common in televised narratives. That encouraged me to think that I was actually accomplishing the kind of contemporary communication I had hoped for. Something as simple as moving out from behind the pulpit can have a profound impact.

3. We might even be moved to use more visual aids for our preaching. Many church buildings in America now have projection screens. I have also seen them in European countries, Malaysia, and Korea. They are presently being used mostly for the words of songs, but I expect to see more and more use of such aids to illustrate and reinforce sermons. Slides or PowerPoint presentations can project pictures, graphs, statistics, and creative combinations of these as reinforcements, enhancements, or illustrations of what we say in sermons.

4. I have suggested to students that they totally re-form the sermon. Instead of twenty to thirty minutes of monologue, why not five or six brief (five-minute) presentations interspersed with music, prayers, scripture readings, and the Lord's supper? I have done this, using stanzas of a hymn to break and apply the sermon. Several students have tried forming the whole hour of worship this way and reported good responses.

5. We can also help people become better listeners. If *shema/ akoe* is the ground out of which faith grows, listening skills are basic to Christian discipleship. My sermon "How Do We Hear?" (appendix 4) is an attempt to be very directive in this regard.

Visual aids, techniques of the theater, dramatic monologues, and other methods can enliven any presentation of the Christian message. But we must keep in mind that the news that we have to proclaim has always been called *good news*, and good news always arrests our attention. Furthermore, our good news comes in the form of an exciting story of our God-in-human-being, a story that only a highly educated, literate preacher could make seem dull.

At the close of a thought-provoking analysis of the role television is playing as the primary storyteller of our society, Quentin Schultze suggests:

[T]he Christian community needs to cultivate its own local storytelling in the face of television's enormous popularity. We cannot be only consumers of others' tales; we must create and pass along our own stories in families, churches, schools and neighborhoods. Not all of us are called to make television programs, but each of us can participate in home-grown narratives that reflect the Christian faith, teach its implications and even amuse. In fact, telling our tales helps us understand how stories work and facilitates sharing our lives more fully with the people we love. When we lose track of our own story, we are ripe for others' propaganda.[8]

Tomorrow's communication demands are upon us today, and we could do much worse than learn from the great communicators of yesterday—learn to use our whole minds, bodies, surroundings, and cultures to lead people to experience the sounds, the sights, the tastes, the smells, the feel, and the emotions of God's story. Such total communication invites total participation of the congregation. Such total communication goes well beyond explaining the truth; it proceeds to invite people to experience the One who is the Truth. This word of truth should be heard at all levels of human consciousness so that we can begin again to live in Christ as the earliest Christians did. Let us pray that the fundamental shift in the structures of human understanding that we are now experiencing will cause not a loss of Christian consciousness, but rather a restoration of the consciousness that was in the early church—a consciousness of total involvement in the reality of God. Then preachers and other Christians will be able to echo the early testimony "We have seen the Lord" (Jn. 20:25b). Then we can all begin to understand what the Lord meant when he said, "Blessed are those who have not seen and yet have come to believe" (Jn. 20:29b).

Our task then is not to explain the gospel; it is not to describe the gospel; it is not even to contextualize the gospel. Our task is to *actualize* the gospel so that people can do more than just listen to it; our task is to help people to enter into it: to eat Jesus' body, to drink his blood, to be baptized into him, to participate in the praise

---

[8]Quentin Schultze, *Redeeming Television: How TV Changes Christians—How Christians Can Change TV* (Downers Grove, Ill.: InterVarsity Press, 1992), 59.

of the Creator, to be in Christ, and in that incarnation to perform the gospel. The only way I know to accomplish this task is to communicate the gospel in such a way that Paul's description of his preaching in Galatia becomes descriptive of our preaching: "Before your eyes...Jesus was publicly exhibited as crucified" (Gal. 3:1b).

Some Closing Advice

So what is my advice to preachers? It is simple: *Look and listen before you preach.* Investigate your local culture's communication forms. Discover how schoolchildren learn about their culture: How do they learn about heroes; about great events in history; about what it means to be Japanese, Korean, Romanian, and so on? How do they learn about the significance of their culture in the world? Do they learn by listening? By reading? By singing? By visiting special places? Does art play a role? How about television, film, computers? How much do they get at home? At school?

Then listen to this complex array of human communication in relation to preaching. Does the gospel of Christ fit well into some forms and not into others? Can some be used as preparation for hearing the gospel? Can some be asked to teach Christian ethical principles? Can some be used to motivate Christians to serve God more fully?

Finally we preachers must ask questions of ourselves. What will we feel comfortable trying? How far can we go without seeming insincere or faddish? For the good of the church, we should press ourselves to try some different approaches. We do so not just to be different. We do it to communicate more broadly and deeply the gospel of Jesus.

"What you hear whispered, shout from the housetops!"

I am ending this book not with answers, but rather with questions. The answers you must find for yourselves. I do not preach in your church, but I am convinced that the gospel can be heard better if we preach that old, old story in forms familiar to the people we are trying to reach. The earliest Christians did just that and were phenomenally effective. As we work to restore their approach to preaching, we should find ourselves not mimicking their forms but applying their method, namely, presenting the good news of Jesus Christ in words and forms familiar enough to our hearers that they will hear and permit God to work on every aspect of their lives. Then we can experience once again the gospel that is "the power of God for salvation to everyone who has faith" (Rom. 1:16), for "faith comes from what is heard, and what is heard comes through the word of Christ" (Rom. 10:17).

APPENDIX 1

Radical Trust

This sermon is an attempt to reposition the preacher as part of a dramatic, dialogic presentation of the implications for contemporary Christians of the incarnation of Jesus. It has been preached in a number of different settings: a suburban congregation, a college chapel, a seminary chapel in Japan, and an urban congregation in Japan. The responses varied according to the venue, which indicates that the audience and their setting are vital parts of the communication impact of such a presentation.

Radical Trust

TEXTS:

Philippians 2:5–11
Luke 10:1–20

From behind the pulpit:

There were a few movements that were so important to the early church that they were told about, taught about, and preached about repeatedly and finally written down several times in the New Testament. I want to call your attention to two of these today—two different stories, which seem to fit together, both looking at sending.

The first of these is the sending of God's Son to earth. The second we'll read in a few minutes—Christ's sending of his disciples. Let's hear first Paul's description of the sending of Christ, in Philippians 2:5–11. [READ]

> Let the same mind be in you that was in Christ Jesus, who, though he was in the form of God, did not regard equality with God as something to be exploited, but emptied himself, taking the form of a slave, being born in human likeness. And being found in human form, he humbled himself and became obedient to the point of death—even death on a cross.
>
> Therefore God also highly exalted him and gave him the name that is above every name, so that at the name of Jesus every knee should bend, in heaven and on earth and under the earth, and every tongue should confess that Jesus Christ is Lord, to the glory of God the Father.

1. Let's use our imaginations to visualize the scene.

Picture this: God decides that it is time to send his Son on a mission to earth. God explains this to his Son.

From one side, facing the pulpit:

Christ's Questions	God's Answers
Which of the angels should I take?	Sorry, no angels.
How big/glorious should I appear?	Sorry, you begin as a baby and remain in human form.
Which of my mental powers may I have?	Sorry, you'll be an intelligent, sensitive human, but no fore-knowledge.
How about a halo?	Only yourself as a vehicle for my word.
Can't I carry anything?	Only a cross!

TRUST ME. [PAUSE]

Behind the pulpit again:

Thirty years later we find Jesus instructing some disciples. [READ Luke 10:1–16.]

> After this the Lord appointed seventy others and sent them on ahead of him in pairs to every town and place where he himself intended to go. He said to them, "The harvest is plentiful, but the laborers are few; therefore ask the Lord of the harvest to send out laborers into his harvest. Go on your way. See, I am sending you out like lambs into the midst of wolves. Carry no purse, no bag, no sandals; and greet no one on the road. Whatever house you enter, first say, 'Peace to this house!' And if anyone is there who shares in peace, your peace will rest on that person; but if not, it will return to you. Remain in the same house, eating and drinking whatever they provide, for the laborer deserves to be paid. Do not move about from house to house. Whenever you enter a town and its people welcome you, eat what is set before you; cure the sick who are there, and

say to them, 'The kingdom of God has come near to you.' But whenever you enter a town and they do not welcome you, go out into its streets and say, 'Even the dust of your town that clings to our feet, we wipe off in protest against you. Yet know this: the kingdom of God has come near'…Whoever listens to you listens to me, and whoever rejects you rejects me, and whoever rejects me rejects the one who sent me.

2. Let's use our imaginations to visualize the heart of the scene.

Picture this: Christ decides to send seventy disciples on a mission. He explains this to his disciples.

From the other side, facing the pulpit:

Their Questions	Christ's Answers
How much money should we take?	Sorry, no money—not even a purse.
We'll just get our staffs.	Sorry, nothing for protection.
I'll get my shoes.	Sorry, no shoes.
Well, how about a coat?	Sorry, no extra clothing.
We'll certainly need begging bags!	Sorry, no bags either.
You mean we go empty-handed?	You have only yourselves and my word.
Can't we carry anything?	Only a cross!

TRUST ME. [PAUSE]

Behind the pulpit again:

3. The story, of course, doesn't end there. [READ vv. 17–20]

The seventy returned with joy, saying, "Lord, in your name even the demons submit to us!" He said to them, "I watched Satan fall from heaven like a flash of lightning. See, I have given you authority to tread on snakes and scorpions, and over all the power of the enemy; and nothing will hurt you. Nevertheless, do not rejoice at this, that the spirits submit to you, but rejoice that your names are written in heaven."

Can you catch their excitement?

"It was scary, but you told us to trust you and we did. And WOW!"

Triumph Results from Radical Trust

4. And do you remember Paul's description of the rest of the story?

Jesus went home on the other side of his humility and death. God exalted him. And so will everybody else sooner or later.

Triumph Results from Radical Trust

5. Can you imagine one more scene?

Picture this: Christ decides he needs people for a special mission. He calls us and explains what he needs us to do right here at home.

From the aisle in the congregation, facing the pulpit:

Our Questions	Christ's Answers
Is there a budget item for that?	Just trust.
Where will the money come from?	Just trust.
Who's going to help?	Just trust.
Where do I get the training?	Just trust.
You mean we go empty-handed?	You have my word.
Can't we carry anything?	Only a cross.

TRUST ME!

Back behind the pulpit:

6. The rest of this story is still ahead of us, but one thing is certain:

In an economy obsessed with financial security,
In a culture centered on possessions and power,

We Christians should hear the real message
of Christ's advent—
Only radical trust in God will bring us to
the ultimate triumph,
TRIUMPH RESULTS FROM RADICAL TRUST!

APPENDIX 2
Performing the Gospel

The overriding aim of this sermon was to communicate in a way that would help the hearers to experience the good news of the forgiveness of sin. To accomplish this, I decided to repeat a number of times the quotation from Jesus of his assurance of forgiveness to the paralytic. I embedded the statement as well as possible in the source story and asked the congregation to try to hear it as spoken directly to them. In this way, I was not only talking about Jesus performing the gospel, but I was doing just that myself. It seems to have been quite effective.

Performing the Gospel

TEXTS:

Isaiah 43:15–25
Luke 5:17–26
1 Corinthians 2:1–4

TEXT: Highlight the story of Jesus and the paralytic. What do you hear when listening to a report like this, as Jesus performed the gospel for that man and for those listening to him? Do you hear Jesus performing the gospel for *you*?

"Friends, your sins are forgiven you."

Do you hear such a statement very often? I wonder why we don't say it more often—even in church, even in rituals.

How does it make you feel?

Something has happened to change the church's talk. It happened so gradually that very few have noticed. Those who kept to the old ways of talking seem hopelessly out of date. They say and do "strange things."

Of course, as human language changes, we do need to change the way we say some things, but we do not need to quit saying them.

Jesus gave his disciples a special vocabulary:

"The kingdom of God is near."

"Repent and believe the gospel."

"Your sins are forgiven."

"Be healed."

The world has given us its corresponding vocabulary:

> "What you see is what you get."
> (This world is not interested in anything beyond itself.)
> "It doesn't get any better than this."
> (Worldly people want to believe that everything is OK just as it is.)
> (Cf. Self-esteem movement; "I'm OK; You're OK" type books.)
> "Guilt is a state of mind best left to psychiatrists and counselors."
> (Without God, people must find healing within themselves.)
> "Healing is the business of science."
> (Science has accomplished great things in this century, but that doesn't mean that it has ultimate solutions for the eternal reality of human beings.)

In fact, the world's vocabulary has produced:

- Ballooning murder rates.
- Assaults on family stability.
- Child criminals with no remorse.
- Ethnic cleansing with the aid of modern weapons.

Christ's vocabulary produced:

- Communities that cared for all neighbors.
- Strong families committed to one another.
- Generations of people with high ethical standards.
- Nations (although never perfect) with a strong sense of what it means to be human.

It is time for us to say no to the words of the world and again to say and do (perform) the gospel.

"The kingdom of God is near." Live so that people see us making decisions based on a power far beyond the human "bottom line." Think of a married couple where one asks, "How can she put up with somebody like me?"

"Repent and believe the gospel." Recognize the terrible reality of sin, but act on the faith that Jesus died and rose again to overcome it. Only as we live with that reality will we begin again to evangelize our neighbors.

"Your sins are forgiven." Lay our burdens of guilt at the Savior's feet so that we can forgive others. Gaither song:

"Forgiven, I repeat it, I'm forgiven.

Clean before my Lord I freely stand.

Forgiven, I can dare forgive my brother.

Forgiven, I reach out to take your hand."[1]

"Be healed." Show that the circumstances of life do not master us because our Master sooner or later heals all our diseases.

Here I illustrate with a personal story of Carrie Edwards and the wild blueberries. The elderly, poor, crippled woman picked, cleaned, and carried several gallons of wild blueberries to give to me as a going-away gift. She mastered the circumstances of her life to give to others.

We won't turn even ourselves around overnight. "The world is too much with us." But with the Lord's help we can know that we are forgiven. With God's help we can stand up and walk. And with God's help we can speak and act in such a way as to bring people to the feet of Jesus so that they, too, can hear, through his church the words, **"Friends, your sins are forgiven you...Stand up and walk."**

---

[1]William J. and Gloria Gaither, "I Am Loved," Gaither Music Co., 1978. Used by permission.

APPENDIX 3
Not "Only Human"

SERMON TEXT:

John 1:1–18

1. When do you use the statement, "After all, I'm only human"?
   a. Time for response from congregation.
   b. Reflect with the congregation about what that means and why we say it when we do.

2. In our sermon text, John refers to the beginning, when God saw that it was *very good*. This strong, positive evaluation comes only after the creation of the first humans.
   a. To use humanity as an excuse is an insult to the work of the Creator.
   b. God made us as the crown of creation—"very good."

3. John also refers to the incarnation: "The Word became flesh."
   a. The Creator became human!
   b. God has shown us in Jesus what it means to be human.
   c. Can you imagine Jesus saying, "After all, I'm only human"?
   d. To be human is to be like Jesus.

4. But John also points out that Christ came to give believers "power to become children of God."
   a. So we Christians are not "only human."
   b. We are human children of God.
   c. We are born not only of the flesh but also of the will of God.
   d. Born again! Born from above! This is indeed good news!

5. Paul puts it another way: "You are God's temple," he says, and "God's Spirit dwells in you" (1 Cor. 3:16).

Fred Craddock's story about Governor Hooper fits here:

Craddock tells of a time when he and his wife were enjoying a quiet, private meal in a restaurant with a marvelous view of the Tennessee mountains, when they were interrupted by an elderly man.

When the man found out that Fred was a preacher he insisted on telling his preacher story—but this one was different. It was about a little boy growing up in a small town in what we now call a single-parent home. He was nearly paranoid with the fear that he was branded as illegitimate and therefore as no good.

However, he was fascinated by the bearded preacher at the local church, so he attended services when he could, sitting in the back so he could escape before anybody else left. One Sunday he tarried too long and was caught in the press of the crowd going to the door. As he got to the preacher, the old prophet caught him by the shoulder and said, "Young man, whose child are you?" Expecting ridicule, the boy tried to wriggle away, but the preacher looked at him and said, "I perceive that you are a child of the King. Go out and claim your inheritance."

Fred then recalled his father talking about a poor, fatherless child who grew up to be governor of Tennessee, and he mentioned that to the old man, who then introduced himself as that very person.

If we know whose child we really are, "only human" will never be an excuse for not becoming what our heavenly Father intends for us.

APPENDIX 4
How Shall We Hear?

I am a professor of preaching. Isn't that impressive? I'm impressed. In fact, I am intimidated. Can you imagine what it's like to be introduced as a professor of preaching and then be expected to preach? Well, instead of preaching at you today, I have decided to talk with you about preaching—specifically about listening to preaching.

For this purpose I chose the reading from Isaiah 6, one of my favorite passages from the Bible, ranking up there with Isaiah 40, Psalm 103, and Romans 8. Isaiah 6:1–8 is one of the most beautiful and moving passages of the Bible. It pictures the young prophet:

- His Confrontation with God (vv. 1–4).
- His Conviction of Sin (v. 5).
- His Cleansing (vv. 6–7).
- His Call (v. 8a).
- His Commitment (v. 8b).

Then comes Isaiah's Commission (vv. 9–13). This is where the tone of the chapter changes. The prophet is sent to a resistant mission field—to people who could not (would not?) perceive.

This is where we confront the simple but profound truth that forms the foundation of what I want to leave with you today: *The effectiveness of preaching depends on the perception of the hearers.*

- Jesus closed most of his parabolic sermons with the sentence, "Let anyone with ears to hear listen." (Mk. 4:9, etc.)
- The apostle Paul indicates in Romans 10:17, "Faith comes from what is heard."
- The book of Revelation repeats the same refrain.

But our question might well be, How do we put ourselves in a position to be real hearers? It should help us to look at some examples of people who heard the word and were changed by the experience. Isaiah heard. Peter heard. Paul heard.

- Paul, when he heard the voice of the Lord, fell to the ground and said, "Who are you, Lord?" (Acts 9:5)
- Peter "fell down at Jesus' knees, saying, 'Go away from me, Lord, for I am a sinful man!'" (Luke 5:8)

173

- Isaiah got off the defensive, confessed his sin, and opened himself to receive (Isaiah 6:5–8).

So must we, if we are to hear the word of God in any sermon or testimony. We must:

1. Get off the defensive. That means to quit our self-justification and its corollary, faultfinding.
2. Confess our sin. Before God's word we are all equal, that is, we "all have sinned."
3. Open ourselves to receive. Alexander Campbell, in his instructions for reading the Bible, said that the interpreter must come within the "circle of understanding," which is a circle whose center is God and whose circumference is determined by the humility of the interpreter. Humility is not thinking about how bad or how useless we are. Humility is the desire not to *use* but to *be used*.

Hearing by a person in this position:

- Is the garden of faith.
- Is the beginning of discipleship.
- Leads to a commission.

How did Isaiah react? "Here am I; send me!" How did he intone that? There are several possibilities, but I like the idea that he was pleading—pleading for God to send him to tell others about God's mercy, which takes a person with unclean lips and cleanses him or her so that those lips can both speak forth God's praise and proclaim God's good news.

Missionaries in foreign fields are often frustrated when people seem not to hear the message that they have carefully communicated. They find that they must first live the gospel before people will listen to it.

The United States is also a mission field, where the gospel of Jesus Christ is a foreign word. You and I had to see the gospel in life before we were able to listen to it with our whole beings. Let us not tire of living and proclaiming the gospel of Christ. Someone out there is nearly ready to hear—perhaps even someone in here.

AMEN.

Bibliography

Abbott, Thomas Kingsmill. *The Epistles to the Ephesians and Colossians.* International Critical Commentary. Edinburgh: T. & T. Clark, 1903, 1977.

Allen, Ronald J. *Contemporary Biblical Interpretation for Preaching.* Valley Forge, Pa.: Judson Press, 1984.

Austin, John L. *How to Do Things with Words.* 2d ed. Edited by J. O. Urmson and Marina Sbisà. Cambridge, Mass.: Harvard University Press, 1975.

——— . "Performative Utterances." In *Philosophical Papers.* Edited by J. O. Urmson and G. J. Warnock. Oxford: Clarendon Press, 1970.

——— . "Performative-Constative." In *The Philosophy of Language.* Edited by John R. Searle. London: Oxford University Press, 1971.

Babin, Pierre. *The New Era in Religious Communication.* Translated by David Smith. Minneapolis: Fortress Press, 1991.

Bailey, Kenneth E. *Poet and Peasant: A Literary Cultural Approach to the Parables in Luke.* Grand Rapids, Mich.: Eerdmans, 1976.

Bainton, Roland. *Here I Stand.* New York: New American Library, 1950.

Barr, David L. "The Apocalypse of John as Oral Enactment." *Interpretation* 40, no. 3 (July 1986): 243–56.

Barr, James. "Revelation through History in the Old Testament and in Modern Theology." *Princeton Seminary Bulletin* 56 (1963): 4–14.

——— . *The Scope and Authority of the Bible.* Philadelphia: Westminster Press, 1980.

Barron, John. "Who Really Rules Russia?" *Readers Digest* (August 1985): 116.

Barth, Karl. *Church Dogmatics.* Vol. 1, part 2, *The Doctrine of the Word of God.* Translated by G. T. Thomson and Harold Knight. Edinburgh: T. & T. Clark, 1963.

——— . *Dogmatics in Outline.* Translated by G. T. Thomson. New York: Harper, 1959.

——— . *The Epistle to the Romans.* Translated by E. C. Hoskyns. Oxford: Oxford University Press, 1975.

Barth, Markus, ed. *Ephesians.* Vol. 34, *The Anchor Bible.* Garden City, N.Y.: Doubleday, 1974.

Bartholomew, Gilbert. "Feed My Lambs: John 21:15–19 as Oral Gospel." *Semeia* 39 (1987): 69–96.

Bausch, William. *Storytelling: Imagination and Faith.* Mystic, Conn.: Twenty-Third Publications, 1984.

Beaudean, John William, Jr. *Paul's Theology of Preaching.* Macon, Ga.: Mercer University Press, 1988.

Beker, J. Christiaan. *Paul the Apostle: The Triumph of God in Life and Thought.* Philadelphia: Fortress Press, 1980.

Berman, Morris. *The Reenchantment of the World.* New York: Bantam, 1985.

Bohren, Rudolf. *Predigtlehre.* Munich: Christian Kaiser Verlag, 1980.

Bond, Stephenson. *Interactive Preaching.* St. Louis: CBP Press, 1991.

Bonhoeffer, Dietrich. *The Cost of Discipleship*. Translated by R. H. Fuller. New York: Macmillan, 1961.

———. *Ethics*. Translated by N. H. Smith. New York: Macmillan, 1962.

Brooks, Phillips. *Lectures on Preaching*. New York: E. P. Dutton, 1877.

Brunner, Emil. *Truth as Encounter*. Translated by A. M. Loos and D. Cairns. Philadelphia: Westminster Press, 1964.

Buechner, Frederick. *Telling the Truth*. New York: Harper & Row, 1977.

Bultmann, Rudolf. *The History of the Synoptic Tradition*. New York: Harper & Row, 1963.

———. *Der Stil der Paulinischen Predigt und die Kynischstoische Diatribe*. Göttingen: Vandenhoeck & Ruprecht, 1910.

Burton-Christie, Douglas. *The Word in the Desert: Scripture and the Quest for Holiness in Early Christian Monasticism*. New York: Oxford University Press, 1992.

Cadbury, Henry J. "Four Features of Lukan Style." In *Studies in Luke-Acts*. Edited by Leander E. Keck and Louis Martyn. London: SPCK, 1976.

Calvin, John. *Commentary on a Harmony of the Evangelists, Matthew, Mark, and Luke*. Grand Rapids, Mich.: Baker Books, 1981.

Cartlidge, David R., and David L. Dungan. *Documents for the Study of the Gospels*. Philadelphia: Fortress Press, 1980.

Clover, Carol. "The Long Prose Form." *Arkiv for Nordisck Filologi* 101 (1986): 10–39.

Craddock, Fred B. *Preaching*. Nashville: Abingdon Press, 1985.

Cranfield, C. E. B. *The Epistle to the Romans*. International Critical Commentary. Edinburgh: T. & T. Clark, 1975.

Culley, Robert. "Oral Tradition and Biblical Studies." *Oral Tradition* 1, no. 1 (January 1986): 30–65.

Davis, Ellen F. *Swallowing the Scroll: Textuality and the Dynamics of Discourse in Ezekiel's Prophecy*. Sheffield, England: Almond Press, 1989.

Dunn, James D. G. *Romans 1—8*, Word Biblical Commentary 38A. Dallas: Word Books, 1988.

Ebeling, Gerhard. *Word and Faith*. Translated by James W. Leitch. Philadelphia: Fortress Press, 1963.

Ellison, Robert H. *The Victorian Pulpit: Spoken and Written Sermons in Nineteenth-Century Britain*. Selinsgrove, Pa.: Susquehanna University Press, 1998.

Fant, Clyde. *Worldly Preaching*. Nashville: Thomas Nelson, 1975.

Farmer, H. H. *The Servant of the Word*. Digswell Place, England: James Nisbet & Co., 1941.

Fitzmyer, Joseph A. *The Gospel According to Luke I—IX*. Vol. 28, *The Anchor Bible*. Garden City, N.Y.: Doubleday 1981.

Foley, John Miles, ed. *Oral-Formulaic Theory: A Folklore Casebook*. New York: Garland Publishing, 1990.

———. *Oral-Formulaic Theory and Research: An Introduction and Annotated Bibliography*. New York: Garland Publishing, 1985.

———. *Oral Tradition in Literature: Interpretation in Context*. Columbia: University of Missouri Press, 1986.

——— . *The Theory of Oral Composition: History and Methodology (Folkloristics)*. Indianapolis: Indiana University Press, 1988.

——— . *Traditional Oral Epic: The Odyssey, Beowulf, and the Serbo-Croatian Return Song*. Los Angeles: University of California Press, 1990.

Fore, William F. *Mythmakers: Gospel, Culture, and the Media*. New York: Friendship Press, 1990.

Gadamer, Hans-Georg. *Truth and Method*. Translated by G. Borden and J. Cumming. New York: Seabury Press, 1975.

Geest, Hans van der. *Presence in the Pulpit*. Atlanta: John Knox Press, 1982.

Gerhardsson, Birger. *Memory and Manuscript: Oral Tradition and Written Transmission in Rabbinic Judaism and Early Christianity*. Acta Seminarii Neotestamentici Upsaliensis, vol. 22. Lund: C. K. Gleerup, 1961.

——— . "The Narrative Meshalim in the Synoptic Gospels." *New Testament Studies* 34 (1988): 339–63.

——— . *The Origins of the Gospel Traditions*. Philadelphia: Fortress Press, 1979.

Graham, William A. *Beyond the Written Word: Oral Aspects of Scripture in the History of Religion*. Cambridge: Cambridge University Press, 1987.

Hardon, John A. "The Miracle Narratives in the Acts of the Apostles." *Catholic Biblical Quarterly* 16, no. 3 (July 1954): 308f.

Harris, William V. *Ancient Literacy*. Cambridge, Mass.: Harvard University Press, 1989.

Harvey, John D. *Listening to the Text: Oral Patterning in Paul's Letters*. Grand Rapids, Mich.: Baker Books, 1998.

Hauck, Friedrich. "Parable." In *Theological Dictionary of the New Testament*. Edited by Gerhard Friedrich and Gerhard Kittel. Vol. 5. Grand Rapids, Mich.: Eerdmans, 1979.

Hawkins, John C. *Horae Synopticae: Contributions to the Study of the Synoptic Problem*. Grand Rapids, Mich.: Baker Books, 1968.

Hengel, Martin. *Acts and the History of Earliest Christianity*. Translated by John Bowden. Philadelphia: Fortress Press, 1979.

Hill, David. *New Testament Prophecy*. Atlanta: John Knox Press, 1979.

Käsemann, Ernst. *An die Römer*. Tübingen: J. C. B. Mohr, 1974.

Kelber, Werner H. *The Oral and the Written Gospel: The Hermeneutics of Speaking and Writing in the Synoptic Tradition, Mark, Paul, and Q*. Philadelphia: Fortress Press, 1983.

Kennedy, George A. *New Testament Interpretation Through Rhetorical Criticism*. Chapel Hill: University of North Carolina Press, 1984.

King, Thomas M. *Enchantments: Religion and the Power of the Word*. Kansas City, Mo.: Sheed & Ward, 1989.

Küng, Hans. *Christsein*. Munich: Deutscher Taschenbuch Verlag, 1974.

Lohr, Charles. "Oral Techniques in the Gospel of Matthew." *Catholic Biblical Quarterly* 23 (1961): 403–35.

Long, Thomas G. *The Witness of Preaching*. Louisville: Westminster/John Knox Press, 1989.

Longenecker, Richard. *Biblical Exegesis in the Apostolic Period.* Grand Rapids, Mich.: Eerdmans, 1975.

Lord, Albert Bates. *Epic Singers and Oral Tradition.* Ithaca, N.Y.: Cornell University Press, 1991.

—— . *The Singer of Tales.* Cambridge, Mass.: Harvard University Press, 1960.

Lowry, Eugene L. *The Homiletical Plot.* Atlanta: John Knox Press, 1980.

McClure, John S. "Conversation and Proclamation: Resources and Issues." *Homiletic* 22, no. 1 (Summer 1997): 1–13.

—— . *The Round-Table Pulpit: Where Leadership and Preaching Meet.* Nashville: Abingdon Press, 1995.

McKitterick, Rosamond. *The Uses of Literacy in Early Medieval Europe.* New York: Cambridge University Press, 1992.

Macquarrie, John. *Twentieth-Century Religious Thought.* New York: Charles Scribner's Sons, 1981.

Magness, J. Lee. *Sense and Absence: Structure and Suspension in the Ending of Mark's Gospel.* Atlanta: Scholars Press, 1986.

Marshall, I. H. *The Gospel of Luke: A Commentary on the Greek Text.* New International Greek Testament Commentary. Grand Rapids, Mich.: Eerdmans, 1978.

Martin, Ralph. *Reconciliation: A Study of Paul's Theology.* Atlanta: John Knox Press, 1981.

Meyer, Ben F. *Jesus and the Oral Gospel Tradition.* Sheffield, England: JSOT Press, 1991.

Meyers, Robin R. *With Ears to Hear: Preaching as Self-Persuasion.* Cleveland: Pilgrim Press, 1993.

Miller, Robert M. *Harry Emerson Fosdick: Preacher, Pastor, Prophet.* New York: Oxford University Press, 1985.

Moltmann, Jürgen. *Crucified God: The Cross of Christ as the Foundation and Criticism of Christian Theology.* Translated by R. A. Wilson and John Bowden. New York: Harper & Row, 1974.

Nanos, Mark D. *The Mystery of Romans: The Jewish Context of Paul's Letter.* Minneapolis: Fortress Press, 1996.

Neusner, Jacob. "The Rabbinic Traditions About the Pharisees Before 70 A.D." *Journal of Jewish Studies* 22 (1971): 1–18.

Niebuhr, Reinhold. *Leaves from the Notebook of a Tamed Cynic.* San Francisco: Harper & Row, 1980.

Norris, Kathleen. *The Cloister Walk.* New York: Riverhead Books, 1996.

Nygren, Anders. *Agape and Eros.* Translated by P. S. Watson. Philadelphia: Westminster Press, 1953.

Ong, Walter J. *Interfaces of the Word: Studies in the Evolution of Consciousness and Culture.* Ithaca, N.Y.: Cornell University Press, 1977.

—— . *Orality and Literacy.* New York: Methuen, 1982.

—— . *The Presence of the Word: Some Prolegomena for Culture and Religious History.* New Haven, Conn.: Yale University Press, 1967; Minneapolis: University of Minnesota Press, 1981.

———— . *Rhetoric, Romance, and Technology.* Ithaca, N.Y.: Cornell University Press, 1971.

Palmer, Richard E. *Hermeneutics.* Evanston, Ill.: Northwestern University Press, 1969.

Palmeri, Anthony J. "Ramism, Ong, and Modern Rhetoric." In *Media, Consciousness, and Culture.* Edited by Bruce E. Gronbeck, Thomas J. Farrell, and Paul A. Soukup. Newbury Park, Calif.: Sage Publications, 1991.

Petrey, Sandy. *Speech Acts and Literary Theory.* New York: Routledge, 1990.

Prigogine, Ilya, and Isabelle Stenger. *Order Out of Chaos.* New York: Bantam, 1984.

Rad, Gerhard von. *Old Testament Theology.* New York: Harper & Row, 1962.

Resner, Andre, Jr. *Preacher and Cross: Person and Message In Theology and Rhetoric.* Grand Rapids, Mich.: Eerdmans, 1999.

Ricoeur, Paul. *Essays on Biblical Interpretation.* Philadelphia: Fortress Press, 1980.

Riesner, Rainer. *Jesus als Lehrer: Eine Untersuchung zum Ursprung der Evangelien-überlieferung.* Tübingen: J. C. B. Mohr, 1988.

———— . "Jesus as Preacher and Teacher." In *Jesus and the Oral Gospel Tradition.* Edited by Henry Wansbrough. Sheffield, England: JSOT Press, 1991.

Robbins, Vernon. *Jesus the Teacher: A Socio-Rhetorical Interpretation of Mark.* Philadelphia: Fortress Press, 1984.

Robinson, J. A. T. *Redating the New Testament.* London: SCM, 1976.

Robinson, Wayne, ed. *Journeys Toward Narrative Preaching.* New York: Pilgrim Press, 1990.

Sanders, James. *God Has a Story Too: Sermons in Context.* Philadelphia: Fortress Press, 1979.

Schlier, Heinrich. *Der Römerbrief.* Freiburg: Herder, 1977.

Schultze, Quentin. *Redeeming Television: How TV Changes Christians—How Christians Can Change TV.* Downers Grove, Ill.: InterVarsity Press, 1992.

———— , ed. *American Evangelicals and the Mass Media.* Grand Rapids, Mich.: Academie Books, 1990.

———— , and Roy Anker. *Dancing in the Dark: Youth, Popular Culture, and the Electronic Media.* Grand Rapids, Mich.: Eerdmans, 1991.

Schweizer, Eduard. *The Good News According to Mark.* Translated by Donald H. Madvig. Atlanta: John Knox Press, 1970.

Shields, Bruce E. "The Areopagus Sermon as a Model for Apologetic Preaching." In *Faith in Practice: Studies in the Book of Acts.* Edited by David A. Fiensy and William D. Howden. Tübingen: European Evangelistic Society, 1996.

———— . *Romans.* Cincinnati: Standard, 1988.

Steimle, Edmund, Morris Niedenthal, and Charles Rice. *Preaching the Story.* Philadelphia: Fortress Press, 1980.

Stott, John R. W. *Between Two Worlds.* Grand Rapids, Mich.: Eerdmans, 1982.

———— . *Christian Counter-Culture: The Message of the Sermon on the Mount.* Downers Grove, Ill.: InterVarsity Press, 1978.

Stuhlmacher, Peter. *Das Evangelium von der Versöhnung in Christas*. Stuttgart: Calwer Verlag, 1979.

———, ed. *The Gospel and the Gospels*. Grand Rapids, Mich.: Eerdmans, 1991.

Sweet, Leonard I., ed. *Communication and Change in American Religious History*. Grand Rapids, Mich.: Eerdmans, 1993.

Thielicke, Helmut. *The Evangelical Faith*. Vol. 2. Grand Rapids, Mich.: Eerdmans, 1977.

Thomas, Rosalind. *Literacy and Orality in Ancient Greece*. Cambridge: Cambridge University Press, 1992.

Vansina, Jan. *Oral Tradition as History*. Madison: University of Wisconsin Press, 1985.

Wansbrough, Henry, ed. *Jesus and the Oral Gospel Tradition*. Sheffield, England: JSOT Press, 1991.

Ward, Richard. *Speaking from the Heart: Preaching with Passion*. Nashville: Abingdon Press, 1992.

Wilkens, Ulrich. *Der Brief an die Römer*. EKKNT, vol. 2. Zurich: Benziger/ Neukirchener Verlag, 1980.

Willimon, William. *The Intrusive Word: Preaching to the Unbaptized*. Grand Rapids, Mich.: Eerdmans, 1994.

Wills, Garry. *Lincoln at Gettysburg: The Words that Remade America*. New York: Touchstone, 1992.

Wingren, Gustav. *Theology in Conflict*. Translated by E. H. Wahlstrom. Philadelphia: Muhlenberg Press, 1958.

Scripture Index

Subject Index